The New Thought Bible Series

Hidden Messages Beyond the Words

New Thought
Exodus

Dr. Don Welsh

by

Reverend Donald Errol Welsh, D.D.

DEDICATION

In memory of Rev. Robert Scott, D.D., R.Sc.D.,
who knew I'd be a minister before I knew it, and who's school of ministry was
in the right place at the right time

Dr. Don Welsh

Introduction

As with all sacred literature, the Bible can be studied from several perspectives including historical, literal, literary, religious and symbolic.

New Thought Exodus looks at the metaphors, allegories and symbolism in the stories, sayings, places and characters of the second book of the Bible, in order to decipher the symbolical meanings between the lines. The interpretations contained in these writings are suggestions gleaned from a metaphysical point of view based upon my studies and insights as a long-time New Thought minister, teacher and student.

Throughout *New Thought Exodus,* I rely heavily on the exhaustive research compiled in the Unity publications, *The Metaphysical Bible Dictionary* and *Mysteries of Genesis* both written by Charles Fillmore. Many of Fillmore's metaphysical definitions are much too extensive to include here, so I refer the reader to these excellent resources whenever there is a desire for further enumeration.

Additionally, I owe my understanding of New Thought Principles to the study of *The Science of Mind* and other books by American philosopher and founder of Religious Science, Ernest Holmes. Dr. Robert Scott was my primary Science of Mind teacher and his influence is definitely present in my choice of words and explanation of New Thought concepts.

I offer my viewpoint as one possible interpretation, recognizing that there are undoubtedly as many perspectives as there are readers of the Bible. The words, parables, poetry and prose in the Book have various meanings for all of us.

Exodus is the story of the Hebrew people as they traveled out of bondage to freedom on their way to the promised land. It is also a continuation of an understanding of the Principles of New Thought. We travel out of a limited historical perspective into a consciousness of freedom and an explanation of the metaphysics of the Bible.

As with "New Thought Genesis," I tell the stories of Exodus in the present tense in order to bring them into today's experience. Exodus is now. I have retained the verse numbers that align with traditional versions for ease in comparing my interpretation with the originals.

Let this story of freedom inspire you to delve further into New Thought, and to find inspiration, insight and provocative material from which you will draw your own conclusions. May you be stimulated to push back the boundaries of your spiritual awareness as you uncover the hidden meanings and use *New Thought Exodus* for your own growth, applying the ideas to enhance your everyday life.

Dr. Don Welsh

Exodus – Journey to Freedom

Chapter 1

These are the names (the nature) of Israel's offspring, who came into Egypt (entered the nature of the subconscious mind and a focus on the material substance). The nature of those listed are of the consciousness of Jacob (mental) or Israel (ISIS-RA-EL or God as feminine, masculine and androgynous principle, therefore spiritual consciousness). The household (consciousness) of Israel are:

2. Reuben (discerning faith), Simeon (obedience), Levi (unity and love) and Judah (praise, inspiration, and Life force),

3. Issachar (zeal), Zebulun (order and balance), and Benjamin (active faith),

4. Dan (judgment), Naphtali (strength), Gad (power) and Asher (wisdom).

5. All of the offspring of the mental and spiritual nature of Jacob are 70 persons (completion). Joseph (imagination) is already in Egypt (the subconscious and material state.

6. Joseph and all his brothers make their transition. (Enter a spiritual state, leaving behind the material consciousness.)

7. While in Egypt, the consciousness of the spiritual and mental nature expands and grows exceedingly strong. The families of Israel (many faculties of mind) expand.

8. New pharaohs or kings of Egypt come into power. They are not acquainted with Joseph and all he has done. They are unfamiliar with the spiritual nature.

9. Pharoah says to his people, "Let's deal with these people of the children of Israel. They're more numerous and stronger than we are.

10. "Let's control them before it's too late. If we were to be at war, they would likely side with the enemies and drive us out of our own land."

11. Therefore, they appoint cruel taskmaster's over the Israelites. They give the Israelites hard work to do building cities with storehouses. The names of the pharoahs are Pithom and Ramses both reflecting a fear of loss of the material.

12. But the more the Israelites are oppressed, the more they multiply and grow stronger. What the Egyptians put out seems to come back to them, which really upsets the Egyptians.

13. So, the Egyptians escalate the oppression.

14. The Egyptians are bitter about the hard work, mixing mortar, carrying heavy bricks and toiling in the fields. They are doing rigorous work.

15. In an effort to stop the expansion and growth of the Israelites, the king of Egypt comes up with another plan. He talks to the Egyptian midwives Puah and Shoprah, those who are shining light on the situation and giving birth to new spiritual thoughts.

16. The king says, "When you aid in the birth of Hebrew boys, I want you to kill them, but if it's a girl, let her live.

17. But the midwives listen to Spirit and disobey the king, letting the baby boys live.

18. The king is not happy about it and questions the midwives. "Why are you letting the boys live?

19. The ladies claim that the Hebrew women are not like Egyptian women in that they deliver babies so fast, that the midwives don't have a chance to do their job.

20. God is good to the midwives since they are in alignment with goodness. And the Israeli people continue to multiply and grow strong.

21. Because of their actions, the midwives are blessed with families of their own.

22. So, Pharaoh demands that all the people, "Cast every son into the river and save every daughter, keeping them alive."

Chapter 2

A man who has a consciousness of love and unity (House of Levi) marries a woman with the same consciousness.

2. She has a handsome son and hides him for three months - something's being created.

3. It becomes difficult to hide him, so she puts him in a basket which is sealed to make it waterproof, and lays it in the reeds by the river's bank.

4. And his sister watches over him from a distance.

5. Pharaoh's daughter comes down to the river to bathe, sees the basket and has one of her maidens investigate.

6. Opening the top of the basket, the maiden sees the crying baby and her heart goes out to the boy who, she realizes, is Hebrew.

7. The boy's sister asks Pharaoh's daughter if she would like her to find a mother among the Hebrew women to nurse the boy.

8. Pharaoh's daughter likes the idea, so the sister gets her own mother.

9. Pharaoh's daughter tells the mother to take the child and nurse him and she will pay her for it. So his own mother nurses the boy.

10. The boy grows and his mother takes him to Pharaoh's daughter who

adopts him. She names him Moses saying, "I drew him out of the water."

11. Moses grows up and goes out among the people. He sees the oppression that is happening; an Egyptian beating one of the Hebrew boys, for example.

12. Careful to look around to make sure no one is watching, Moses slays the Egyptian and buries him in the sand.

13. The next day, he goes out among the people and hears two Hebrew men quarreling, one attacks the other. Moses asks him why he is beating him.

14. The man replies, "Who made you a prince and a judge over us? Do you intend to kill me like you killed the Egyptian yesterday?" Moses is afraid, since his actions are already known.

15. Indeed, when Pharaoh hears about it, he plans to kill Moses. However, Moses escapes to the land of Midian (rule and government) and he sits by a well (entrance to the subconscious mind).

16. The priest of Midian has seven daughters who come to the well to draw water and carry it to troughs for watering their father's flock (bring life to thoughts).

17. The shepherds come and drive maidens away. But Moses saves and protects them and waters their flocks.

18. When the maidens go home to their father, Jehro (his excellency) Reuel (inner guide), he asks how they completed their task of watering the flocks so soon.

19. They tell their father about an Egyptian protecting them from the shepherds and watering the flocks.

20. And Reuel tells them to go and invite him to eat bread (the substance of life) with them .

21. Moses enjoys being there and stays with Reuel who gives his daughter Zipporah (like a little bird or swift and free thoughts) to him for a wife.

22. She gives birth to a son, Gershon (stranger/isolation), and Moses says, "I have been a stranger in a strange land." His second son is born and they name him Eleazar (spiritual strength). He says, "For the God of my fathers has helped me and has delivered me from the sword of Pharoah."

23. Eventually, the king of Egypt makes his transition and a more oppressive ruler takes over. So the children of Israel complain and pray.

24. God hears their prayers and in keeping with the covenant with Abraham and because of God's loving nature,

25. God is aware of the situation.

Chapter 3

Moses is feeding flocks (thoughts) belonging to Jethro (his excellence) Reuel, his father in law, the priest of Midian, and leads them into the desert (alone with his thoughts) and to Horeb (the mountain of God).

2. An angel or messenger from God (higher idea) appears to Moses in a flame of fire appearing to come out of the midst of the bush. It appears that the bush is on fire but it doesn't burn the bush (it's not consumed as it burns).

3. Moses thinks, "I will now take a break and look at this great phenomenon, and why the bush is burning but not being consumed by it."

4. Having gotten Moses' attention, the Voice called out to him from within the bush saying "Moses, Moses." And he answers, Here I am,"

5. The Voice warns, "Don't come closer. Take your shoes off of your feet, for the place on which you stand is holy ground.

6. "But wait. There's more!" the Voice says. "I am the God of your father, the God of Abraham, the God of Isaac, and the God of Jacob." And Moses hides his face because he is afraid to look at God.

7. And the "I Am" says, "I have seen the affliction of my people, who are in Egypt, and have heard their cries and know their sorrows.

8. "I have come into the Earth dimension to deliver my people out of the hand of the Egyptians, and to bring them up out of that land (consciousness) to a good and large land, to a land flowing with milk and honey; to the land of the Canaanites (materialistic), Amorites (haughtiness), Hittites (resistance), Perizzites (scattered; unfocused), Hivites (physical or flesh consciousness) and the Jebusites (contention).

9. "The cry of the children of Israel is come to me. And I see the oppression the Egyptians inflict.

10. "Therefore, I will send you to Pharaoh to request that my people be permitted to leave Egypt."

11. And Moses says to God, "Who I am that I should go to Pharaoh and be the one to lead the children of Israel out of Egypt?

12. God says to him, "I will be with you. And this shall be a sign that it is really me that has sent you: When you have brought forth the people out of Egypt, you shall worship me on this mountain."

13. Moses says, "When I go to the children of Israel and say 'The God of my fathers has sent me to you, they shall say to me, 'What is his name?' what shall I say to them?'"

14. And God says to Moses, "I am the living God, the I Am that I Am,

that which is. Thus you shall say to the children of Israel, 'Adonai, the Lord, the Isness has sent me to you'."

15. And God says to Moses, "Thus shall you say to the children of Israel, that you are sent by The Living God of your fathers, the God of Abraham, the God of Isaac, and the God of Jacob. This is my name and nature forever."

16. "Go and gather the elders of Israel together and tell them that the Lord God of your fathers, the God of Abraham, Isaac, and of Jacob appeared to you saying, 'I have surely remembered you and seen that which is done to you in Egypt.'

17. "And I have said, 'I will bring you up out of the affliction of the Egyptians to the land of the Canaanites, Hittites, Amorites, Perizzites, Hivites, Jebusites to a land flowing with milk and honey.

18."'And they shall respond to your voice and you and the elders of Israel shall go to the king of Egypt, and say to him 'Adonai, the Lord God of the Hebrews has appeared to us and now let us go three days journey into the wilderness so we can sacrifice to the Living God.'

19. "And I know the king of Egypt will not let you go, except by force.

20. "So, the Law of Cause and Effect will make all kinds of wonders come to them until finally Pharaoh gives in and lets you go

21. "And I will see that the Egyptians look favorably on my people so when you go, you shall not go empty handed.

22."But every woman shall borrow of her neighbor all the Jewels of silver and gold and all the clothes, and you shall put them on your sons, and on your daughters leaving the Egyptians with none of these things."

Chapter 4

Moses' response is that the people won't believe him or listen to his voice saying that God has not appeared to Moses.

2. What's that in your hand?" God asked. Moses replies, "A staff."

3. "Cast it on the ground," God commands. Moses does as he is told and the staff becomes a serpent. Moses jumps away.

4. God says, "Take it by the tail," which Moses does, and it becomes a staff again.

5. "This is done so they'll believe I appeared to you.

6. "Now put your hand next to your chest." And Moses place his hand on his chest, and when he takes it out, his hand was leprous, appearing as white as snow.

7. God then says, "Put your hand back on your chest." Moses does as told and when he takes it out, it is clean like his other flesh.

8. "If they will not believe you with the first sign, they will believe the second sign.

9. "Yet, if they will not believe both signs or listen to what you tell them, take some water from the river and pour it on dry dirt and the water will turn to blood. The use of masculine energy symbolized by the staff, feminine energy of the heart within the chest, and life force acting on the earth show the power of the Creative Process in action."

10. Moses then tries avoiding the confrontation with Pharaoh by claiming that he stutters and has trouble speaking.

11. God has an answer for that. "Who makes man's mouth? Or who

determines whether a person is deaf, dumb, has keen hearing or good eyesight? Is it not I, the Love and Law of the Universe?

12. "I will be your mouth and speak through you telling you what to say."

13. Moses continues to protest. "Please send someone else. You have the power to send anyone."

14. Moses' stubbornness creates a feeling of separation from God and Moses thinks God is angry. God says, "Your brother Aaron of the tribe of Levi (love and unity) is a good speaker and I know when he steps forward, he'll be glad to see you and open to helping.

15. "Tell him what I told you to say and teach him what I teach you.

16. "Aaron will be your spokesperson to the people. You shall be like my voice speaking through you to him to others.

17. "Take your staff with you to do miraculous signs."

18. Moses returns and speaks to Jethro, his father in law, saying, "Let me go and return to my brothers who are in Egypt and see whether they are still alive." And Jethro says to Moses, "Go in peace."

19. God lets Moses know that all the men in Egypt who wanted to kill him are dead.

20. And Moses has his wife and sons ride on an ass and he starts off for Egypt. He takes his staff.

21. God reminds Moses to perform all the wonders in front of Pharaoh when he gets back to Egypt. God is providing the means by which the resistance Moses will encounter from Pharaoh can be met.

22. God tells Moses to say to Pharaoh, "Thus says the Lord, 'Israel is my first-born son.

23. 'And I say to you, Let my son go, that is, let the families of Israel go, so they may serve my purposes. and if you don't, I'll slay your first-born son'."

24. When Moses is on his way to an inn, the Law of Cause and Effect is about to catch up with him as he had killed a man in Egypt.

25. But Zipporah, (freeing thoughts) performs a circumcision on her son (cleansed the consciousness for the family) saying, "I have a bloody husband." (His karma is cleared).

26. So, he avoids the affects of the Law.

27. God tells Aaron to go into the wilderness and meet Moses, when Moses is still at Mount Horeb. And he goes to Mount Horeb and greets his brother with a kiss.

28. And Moses relates all that God had told him and all the signs that God showed Moses to perform.

29. Moses and Aaron gather all the elders of the children of Israel.

30. And Aaron speaks all the words which the Great I Am had said to Moses, and performs the signs in the presence of the people.

31. And the people believe. They hear that the Lord has remembered the children of Israel and that he had seen their challenges and they kneel down and worship Spirit.

Chapter 5

Afterward, Moses and Aaron go to the palace and tell Pharaoh, "Thus says the Lord God of Israel, 'Let my people go so they may honor me with the full abundance and enjoyment of life."

2. And Pharaoh responds, "Who is the Lord that I should obey his demands to let Israel go? I don't know this Lord and I will not let Israel go."

3. Moses and Aaron say, "The Lord God of the Hebrews has appeared to us; let us go three days journey into the wilderness so we may honor our God and avoid negative results."

4. Pharaoh asked, "What right do you have to allow the people to stop working? Go back to your tasks."

5. He points out the sheer numbers of workers of the consciousness of Israel and what an impact it would cause for them all to stop working.

6. He not only denies their request,

7. But he requires that they supply their own straw to make bricks.

8. And he insists that they keep up the same level of productivity, despite the extra work involved.

9. He says, "Give them more work to do so they don't have time for idle chatter."

10. The taskmasters relay the bad news.

11. "Go find you own straw and you must maintain a high level of completing your work."

12. The people scatter across the land looking for straw. Their unified focus is interrupted.

13. Yet the taskmasters demand that they complete the high level of achievement.

14. They beat the leaders for not reaching their quota of brick making.

15. They complain about it to Pharaoh.

16. The situation is frustrating.

17. Pharaoh argues, "If you have time to go out into the wilderness to honor your God, you must have idle time on your hands.

18. "Go back to work."

19. The leaders of Israel recognize the impossibility of the situation.

20. So, they talk to Moses and Aaron about it.

21. They blame them for making things worse.

22. Moses goes back to God with the problem.

23. He points out that Pharaoh hasn't budged and there has been not progress or improvement.

Chapter 6

God says to Moses that He will show his Power to Pharaoh.

2. He points out that He is the same all-powerful God that has always been.

3. "I am the God who appeared to Abraham, Isaac and Jacob, but even they didn't know my full power.

4."I did promise to give to my people the land of Canaan.

5. "And I am hearing the complaints of the children of Israel.

6. "Therefore, I will bring you out of Egypt and the physical burdens.

7. "I will be your God.

8. "And I will give you the inheritance I promised."

9. Moses relays these words to the people, but they are so caught up in the misery and bondage, that they can't really hear him.

10. Infinite Intelligence speaks to Moses.

11. He tells him to go back to Pharaoh and once again demand that he let the people go.

12. Moses points out that Pharaoh hasn't complied with his requests, thinking maybe it's because of his speech impediment.

13. Still, God charges Moses and Aaron to repeat the request to Pharaoh to let the people go.

14. The new generation of leaders are: The house of Reuben (discerning faith) and Hanoch (higher consciousness than ever), Pallu (distinguished greatness), Hezron (thoughts awaiting full expression), and Carmi (fruitful thoughts).

15. From the house of Simeon (obedience): Jemuel (light of God), Jamin (divine order), Ohad (unity with God), Jachin (loyalty, steadfastness), Zohar (purity), and Shaul (will).

16. The sons of Levi (unity and love) are Gershon (the appearance of resistance to being loving), Kohath (unifying aspect of love) and Merari

(love directed by ignorance and selfishness). Levi lives to the age of one hundred thirty-seven which numerologically reduces to eleven and to two meaning duality.

17. The sons of Gershon (resistance to love) are Libni (purity) and Shimi (receptivity).

18. The offspring of Kohath (unifying) are Amram (related to God), Izhar (spiritual understanding), Hebron (brotherhood) and Uzziel (power of God). Kohath lives to one hundred thirty-three years which is a seven (completion).

19. The sons of Merari are Mahali or Mahli (love that is directed by selfishness) and Mushi (natural love that is sensitive).

20. Amram marries Jokhaber or Jochabed (exalting God) and she gives birth to Aaron (spiritual strength), Moses (drawing out) and (Miriam feminine side of love) and lives to be 137 or 11 which is a 2 or duality.

21. The sons of Izhar (spiritual understanding) are Korah (coldness and unproductiveness), Nepheg (a development in consciousness of understanding) and Zichri (thoughts in spiritual consciousness).

22. The sons of Uzziel (power of God) are Minshael or Mishael (Love and Godlikeness), Elizphan (Inner assurance of divine protection), and Zithri or Sithri (a thought of divine care and protection).

23. Aaron (spiritual strength) marries Elizabeth or Elisheba (full assurance in the feminine or soul consciousness of God's Truth), the dauther of Amminadab (generosity), sister of Nehshon or Nahshon (Divine wisdom), and gives birth to Nadab (presumptuous ruling thoughts of religious consciousness), Abihu (Divine sonship), Eleazar (spritual strength) and Ithamar (a consciousness of victory).

24. The sons of Korah (unifying) are Assir (cold and unproductive),

Hilkanah or Elkanah (Man is of God and from God) and Akensap or Abiasaph (gathers together). These are the families of the Korhites (unifiers to the point of love).

25. Aaron's son, Eleazar (spiritual strength) marries one of the daughters of Putiel (mistaken belief in limitation by God) and gives birth to Phineas or Phinehas (spiritual revelation and power). These are the heads of the households of the Levites.

26. These are the same Aaron and Moses to whom the Lord God says, "Bring out the children of Israel from the land of Egypt (consciousness of bondage)."

27. It was Moses and Aaron who spoke to Pharoah, the king of Egypt.

28. When God had spoken to Moses,

29. Moses had protested

30. Saying that he has trouble speaking, so how could Pharaoh respond?

Chapter 7

The Lord God's voice within Moses tells him that He has made Moses like a god to Pharaoh and Aaron like his prophet.

2. "You shall speak all I command you; and Aaron shall tell Pharaoh to send the children of Israel out of his land.

3. "And I will cause Pharaoh to be stubborn and will cause my signs and wonders in the land of Egypt to be multiplied.

4. "But Pharaoh will not listen to you which will cause my Law to create hard consequences for Egypt but provide the way for the children of

Israel to leave the land.

5. "And the Egyptians will recognize my power."

6. Aaron and Moses do as God commanded.

7. Moses is 80 and Aaron 83, the number of the infinite and the number symbolizing duality; the absolute and the relative.

8. The Lord God says to Moses and Aaron,

9. "If Pharaoh asks for a sign, have Aaron throw his staff to the ground and it will become a serpent, representing the power of the Life Force."

10. So, Moses and Aaron go to Pharaoh and do just that.

11. But Pharaoh calls in his magicians and they do the same trick.

12. And Aaron's serpent swallows up theirs.

13. Still, Pharaoh remains stubborn and denies Moses and Aaron's request.

14. Exactly what the God said would transpire has.

15. God tells Moses to go to Pharaoh again and stand by the river with the serpent.

16. "Tell Pharaoh the Lord God of the Hebrews has sent you saying 'Let my people go so they can serve me in the wilderness'."

17. God tells Moses to strike the water with his staff and it will turn to blood.

18. And the fish will die and stink so the Egyptians won't drink it.

19. "Tell Aaron to strike all the water with his staff so it all turns to blood, even the ponds and pools and streams and even the water in wooden and stone vessels. There'll be blood everywhere throughout Egypt."

20. So, Aaron and Moses do as they are told and sure enough, all the waters turn to blood.

21. And the fish die and smell badly.

22. The Egyptian magicians can do the same trick so it doesn't impress Pharaoh.

23. He remains stubborn about the Hebrews leaving.

24. The Egyptians dig for water since they can't drink the river water.

25. Seven days pass.

Chapter 8

Again God urges Moses to appeal to Pharaoh saying, "Let my people go that they may serve me.

2. "And if you don't, I'll inundate your borders with frogs.

3. "And the river will swarm with frogs, which will enter your house and bedroom and washroom.

4. "And the frogs will leap on you and your people." The amphibious nature of the frogs indicates indecisiveness. Change is difficult. The people want freedom, yet they have been comfortable living in Egypt.

5. God says, "Tell Aaron to lift up his staff over the rivers, streams, and ponds and cause frogs to come upon the land."

6. Aaron does as he is instructed. And the frogs cover the land of Egypt.

7. The Egyptian magicians do the same.

8. Then, Pharaoh calls for Moses and Aaron and requests that they pray to their God to remove the frogs and Pharaoh says, "I will let the people go,"

9. Moses asks Pharaoh to determine a time when he wants the frogs to be removed.

10. Pharaoh says, "Tomorrow." And Moses says, "So be it according to your word, so you'll know how powerful God is.

11. "The frogs will depart from all the waters except the river."

12. And Moses prays.

13. And the frogs die.

14. They gather them together and they stink.

15. When Pharaoh sees that the frogs are gone, he reverts to his old decision to disallow the people to leave.

16. So God tells Moses to have Aaron lift his staff and turn all the dust to lice.

17. The dust becomes lice and covers men and cattle.

18. The Egyptian magicians could do the same thing, but they can't remove the lice.

19. The magicians tell Pharaoh this is God's doing. But still, Pharaoh is belligerent and doesn't listen. The situation is an irritation to all.

20. God says to Moses to catch Pharaoh as he goes to the water to do his daily duty early in the morning and tell him to let the people go.

21. "Tell him that if he refuses, I will send swarms of flies (annoyances) upon him and his people.

22. "I will separate the land of Goshen where my people live, excluding it from the swarms of flies for the purpose of showing Pharaoh my presence and power.

23. "Tomorrow I will create a division between my people and Pharaoh's people as a sign."

24. So, God brings great swarms of flies into Pharaoh's house and the houses of his servants and into the entire land of Egypt.

25. Then Pharaoh calls for Moses and Aaron and asks them to sacrifice to their God to remove the flies.

26. But Moses says, "That wouldn't be proper because if we sacrifice animals that are sacred to Egyptians, they will stone us."

27. "We will journey three days into the wilderness and sacrifice to God, using the creative process."

28. Pharaoh says, "I will let your people go so you can sacrifice to your God in the wilderness, but don't go too far away, and you must pray for me, also."

29. So Moses agrees to pray for Pharaoh and remove the swarms of flies, but insists that Pharaoh keep his agreement this time.

30. So Moses goes out into the wilderness and prays.

31. And God removes the swarms of flies. Not even one remains.

32. But Pharaoh still remains stubborn and won't release the people.

Chapter 9

God tells Moses to go back to Pharaoh and say, "Let my people go that they may serve me.

2. "And if you refuse as you have before,

3."God will attack your cattle which are in the desert and the horses, asses, camels, oxen and the sheep. There will be a severe plague.

4. "And God will keep the cattle of the people of Israel separate so none of them will die."

5. God sets an appointed time the next day to send the plague,

6, And the Law does the thing the next day. But the animals of the Israeli's aren't harmed.

7. Even still, Pharaoh is stubborn.

8. God has another idea. He says to Aaron and Moses to take two hands full of ashes from the furnace and scatter it toward the sky where Pharaoh will see it.

9. "It will become fine dust throughout Egypt causing sores to break out on men and cattle."

10. When they did it, blistering boils formed on men and cattle.

11. And because the Egyptian magicians had boils, they were too uncomfortable to stand before Pharaoh and do the same magic.

12. But Pharaoh doesn't budge.

13. Next, God tells Moses to try again.

14. "This time I'll send a plague on Pharaoh's heart

15. "And strike him and his people with a deadly pestilence;

16. "That's the whole reason Pharaoh is in such a powerful position; everyone will know about this.

17. "So far you have not given in.

18. "So, tomorrow at about this time, I'll send a severe hailstorm worse than Egypt has experienced in its entire history.

19. "So gather together everyone and all their cattle and have them take shelter or the hail will kill them."

20. Everyone who believes it, takes cover and brings their cattle in.

21. Those who don't, leave their servants and cattle outside.

22. God tells Moses to lift up his hand to cause the hail.

23. Moses lifts his staff and Divine Nature sends thunder, hail and lightning.

24. It looks like flaming hail like fire and it is unequaled in history.

25. Every person, animal and object left out of doors is destroyed, even the herbs on the ground and tree in the field.

26. The only place where there is not hail is the land of Goshen where the Israelites live.

27. Then Pharaoh sends for Moses and Aaron and finally admits that he has made a big mistake.

28. He asks for prayer and forgiveness and for the thunder and hail to stop.

29. Moses agrees to raise his hand to stop the storming once he leaves the city.

30. Yet, he knows Pharaoh hasn't learned his lesson yet.

31. He assesses the crop damage: the flax and barley are ruined,

32. But the wheat and rye are alright as they were planted later.

33. As Moses leaves, his signal to God stops the storming.

34. But Pharaoh still hasn't learned his lesson.

35. He violates his agreement one more time.

Chapter 10

The Lord God says to Moses, "Go to Pharaoh again,

2. "So you'll be able to relate all that transpires to prove the power that I am."

3. And Moses and Aaron go to Pharaoh asking how long he's going to fight co-operating with Spirit.

4. They warn him of another plague: locusts swarming throughout Egypt.

5. "They'll be so thick that men won't be able to see the ground. They'll eat all the stuff left from hail damage. They'll eat all the trees.

6. "They'll fill your houses and the houses of all your servants."

7. Pharaoh's servants argued to let the Israelites go. They ask, "How long do we have to put up with them? Don't you realize Egypt is destroyed?"

8. So, Pharaoh sends for Moses and Aaron and asked who all he plans to take with him.

9. Moses replies, "We'll go with our young and with our old, with our sons and daughters, with our flocks and herds. It's a celebration for all of us."

10. God says, "Go ahead take the young and old. But make sure you don't do any evil."

11. And they are driven out of Pharaoh's presence.

12. God tells Moses to lift up his hand to send back the locusts to eat all the herbs that the hail left.

13. Moses lifts his staff and Divine nature sends an east wind all day and night, which brings the locusts in the morning.

14. The locusts swarm and remain in Egypt.

15. They cover the whole land and eat all the vegetation.

16. Pharaoh calls Moses and Aaron before him and confesses his mistakes and his errors against the God of the children of Israel and against the Hebrew people.

17. He asks for forgiveness and for the plague to be removed.

18. Moses goes out from Pharaoh and prays to God.

19. Divine Nature causes a strong west wind which sweeps all the locusts away.

20. But, once again, Pharaoh turns stubborn and won't let the people go.

21. God tells Moses to lift up his hand and cause very thick darkness over the land.

22. Moses lifts his hand and there is thick darkness – extreme negativity.

23. None of the Egyptians can see a thing because of the darkness, lasting three days. But the children of Israel have light in their houses.

24. Pharaoh calls to Moses saying "Go and serve your God, but let your flocks and herds remain here. You can take your little ones."

25. Moses asks for sacrifices to offer God.

26. "We'll also take our cattle with us, just in case we need more sacrifices."

27. Once again, Pharaoh's ego gets in the way and he balks.

28. "Get out of here," warns Pharaoh, "and don't try to see my face

again, or you will die."

29. Moses agrees. "I won't try to see your face again."

Chapter 11

God says, "I'll bring one more plague upon Pharaoh and the Egyptians. Then you should clear out all together.

2. "Speak to your people and tell them to ask their neighbors for silver and gold jewelry."

3. Things are finally going their way. And Moses is highly honored among the servants of Pharaoh.

4. Moses says, "Thus says the Lord: 'About midnight I will go into the midst of Egypt.

5. "'And all the first-born in the land of Egypt shall die, from Pharaoh's son to the lowliest maidservant's son, and even the first- born of all the animals.

6. "' And there shall be great wailing throughout Egypt like never before nor will there be since.

7. "'But of the children of Israel, none will be harmed, not even a dog shall bark against men, so you will know that God discriminates between the Egyptians and Israel.'

8. "And all these servants shall come down to me and bow down to me telling me to get out, both me and my people. And after that, I will go out." And Moses leaves Pharaoh in great anger.

9. And the Lord God says to Moses, "Pharaoh shall not listen to you; which will make me look good."

10. And Moses and Aaron perform all these wonders in front of Pharaoh, but he continues to hold back permission to leave.

Chapter 12

God tells Moses and Aaron,

2. "This month will be the beginning of a new calendar. It shall be the first month of the year to you.

3. "Speak to all the people of Israel. Tell them that on the tenth day of this month, each shall take a lamb for his own household and a lamb for his father's household.

4. "And if the household is to small for a lamb, let him join with his next door neighbor. Take one, depending upon the number in the households.

5. "The lamb shall be without blemish and be a yearling, a lamb or a kid.

6. "Keep it until the fourteenth day of the month and everyone shall kill it at sunset.

7. "Take some of the blood and sprinkle it on the doorposts and the lintel of the houses where they will eat it.

8. "They shall eat the meat in that night, roasted above the fire, with unleavened bread, as it may not have time to rise before leaving Egypt and with bitter herbs to symbolize bitter tears the people have shed.

9. "Don't eat any of it raw or boiled in water. Roast it by fire – its head with the feet and the entrails.

10. "Eat it all that night and if any remains, burn it.

11. "Eat it fully clothed and with your shoes on your feet and staff in your hand, and eat it quickly so you'll be ready to leave. This is God's Passover.

12. "I will pass through the land this night, and all the first-born of the land shall die, both man and animal.

13. "But the blood will be a sign and when I see it, I shall make you glad because I will pass over the house.

14. "This day will be a memorial and a day of celebration to keep forever.

15. "Eat unleavened bread for seven days, removing all leaven from your house the entire time, so you can live fully as an Israelite.

16. "On the first day and the seventh day, have a holy convocation, a sacred gathering, in which no work is done except for any necessary preparation of food.

17. "Observe the feast of the unleavened bread until the evening of the twenty-first day. Continue this feast every year throughout the generations.

18. In the first month, on the fourteenth day of the month at evening, you shall eat unleavened bread until the twenty-first day at evening.

19. There shall be no leavened bread found in your houses for seven days, for whoever eats that which is leavened will not live fully as an Israelite whether a stranger or a native of the land.

20. You shall eat nothing leavened in your households; you shall eat unleavened bread.

21. Moses called all the elders of the children of Israel and said to them, "Hurry and take lambs for yourselves according to the number in your families and kill the pass over lamb.

22. "And take a bunch of hyssop (a plant of the mint family) and dip it in the blood of the lamb and sprinkle the lintel and the door posts with the blood. None of you shall go out of the door until morning.

23. "For the Lord God will pass through to attack the Egyptians. And when he sees blood on the doorposts and lintel, the Lord will bring joy to your doors and will not allow destruction to come into your houses.

24. "You shall observe this rite forever.

25. "And when you enter the land which the Lord will give you, you shall continue this practice.

26. "And when your children ask the meaning of this observance,

27. "You shall say, 'it is the sacrifice of the Lord's Passover, who brought joy to the homes of the children of Israel when he attacked the Egyptians and preserved our houses'." The people bow their heads and worship the Adonai.

28. The children of Israel do as God instructs.

29. At midnight, God's Law of Cause and Effect brings harm to the first-born of the Egyptians, from the first-born of Pharaoh to the first-born of the captive who is in the prison and all the first-born of cattle.

30. Pharaoh gets up in the night and he and all the servants and all the Egyptians discover the attacks and there is great wailing.

31. Pharaoh contacts Moses and Aaron that very night and says to them, "You and the children of Israel, get up and get out from among

my people, and go and serve your Lord like you said.

32. "Also, take your flocks and herds and be gone. Also, bless me."

33. The Egyptians urge their people to get the children of Israel out of the land of Egypt in a hurry, saying, "We'll all die."

34. The children of Israel take their kneading dough before it is leavened and their cold kneading dough wrapped up and placed on their shoulders.

35. And the children of Israel do as Moses instructs and they borrow the Egyptians silver and gold and clothing.

36. God makes it easy for the Egyptians to lend their possessions to the Israelites so that they were stripped.

37. Then the children of Israel travel from Ramses, meaning "sun of the son" - where the misuse of the identity of sonship by Pharaoh causes plagues - to Succoth, meaning a temporary dwelling place, which could be construed to symbolize the physical body which is also temporary on the grand scale of life. The Israelites travel on foot with some six hundred thousand men plus their little ones. Numerologically, a six falls short of the complete journey.

38. A mixed multitude goes with them and their flocks, herds, and many cattle.

39. They bake unleavened bread on a griddle, using the dough they have with them. They had not been able to leaven it or make it into loaves because the Egyptians drove them out. They hadn't been able to bring other provisions with them, either.

40. Now, the number of years the Israelites had dwelt in Egypt was four hundred-thirty years which totals seven. They were complete in living

there.

41. It happens that on that day, the spiritual essence or hosts, leave Egypt.

42. This night is to be observed throughout all generations.

43. God tells Moses and Aaron that it is a rule of the observation of Passover that no foreigner shall partake of it.

44. But any servant whose consciousness is cleansed (circumcised) shall be able to eat of the meal.

45. An alien and a hired servant shall not eat it.

46. "Don't take any of the meat out of the house. Don't break any of the bones.

47. "Everyone who is an offspring of Israel shall have the meal.

48. "A traveler may keep the Passover with you as long as every male of his household has a cleansed consciousness (circumcised).

49. "There'll be one law for the natives and strangers among you."

50. All the children of Israel follow these guidelines communicated through Moses and Aaron.

51. The Lord God brings all of the children of Israel and their inner spiritual guides out of Egypt on this day.

Chapter 13

God speaks to Moses.

2. "Dedicate every first-born child and animal to me."

3. Moses reminds the people to remember their journey out of Egypt.

4. It is the month of Abib.

5. It will commemorate the entry into the land of milk and honey that God has promised.

6. "On the seventh day there'll be a festival honoring God.

7. "For seven days, there'll be unleavened bread and then leavening on the seventh day.

8. "Tell your sons this is done because God brought you out of Egypt this day.

9. "It will be a memorial.

10. "Keep the tradition from year to year.

11. "It will be complete when God takes you into the land of Canaan, the promised land.

12. "Every first-born son and male animal shall belong to God.

13. "Every first-born male of your cattle shall be redeemed with a lamb or if you don't wish to redeem it, you must kill it. Also, every first-born son you must redeem.

14. "And when your son asks you about this, explain that God brought us out of Egypt with his powerful force, freeing us from bondage.

15. "Tell them how stubborn Pharaoh was and how the Law of Cause

and Effect killed their first born sons and male animals and that's why I sacrifice to the Law and redeem my first son. Explain that the Law returns God's blessings upon you that way.

16. "It's a token gesture that you pass on to each generation."

17. When Pharaoh lets the people go, God does not lead them the shortest way, near the Philistines because it might be frightening for the children of Israel to see war and they might want to return to Egypt.

18. But God leads them by the Reed Sea.

19. And Moses is taking the bones of Joseph with him because the children of Israel had promised Abraham they would.

20. They travel from Succoth and encamp at Etham (negative consciousness; desolation).

21. But Spirit guides and uplifts them showing up as a pillar of cloud by day and a pillar of fire, to give them light, by night.

22. Spirit never fails to guide them.

Chapter 14.

Adonai speaks to Moses.

2. "Speak to the children of Israel to turn toward Kheritha which is dry at low tide between Magdol and the sea and encamp there by the sea.

3. "Pharaoh will observe that the Israelites don't know the land. They're trapped between the wilderness and the sea."

4. The Lord God says to Moses, "Pharaoh will change his mind and chase

after your people, but I'll triumph over him and his army and the Egyptians will know that I am God."

5. Pharaoh realizes it was a mistake to let all their servants, the children of Israel, leave the country.

6. He has his chariots prepared to pursue the Israelites.

7. He takes 600 chosen chariots.

8. And goes after the people.

9. He and his horsemen and chariots overtake the children of Israel at Kheritha, next to the sea.

10. They see them coming and pray.

11. They question Moses' leadership, asking "Why did you take us out of Egypt?

12. "It would have been better for us to serve the Egyptians than to die in the wilderness."

13. Moses says, "Don't be afraid; watch what God will do! You won't see these Egyptians again.

14. "God will fight for you. Hold your peace."

15. God tells Moses to have the people move their feet.

16. "And as for you," he says, "Lift up your staff, stretch out your arms over the sea of reeds and the water will appear to divide and the children of Israel will walk across on dry ground.

17. "When Pharaoh tries to follow, I will triumph over his army, his

chariots and his horsemen.

18. "And the Egyptians shall know that I am God."

19. An angel, Spiritual Energy, goes in front of and behind the children of Israel,

20. The pillar of the cloud of Divine Goodness is between them and the Egyptians as a protective barrier.

21. And it gives light to the Israelites all night.

22. As Moses lifts his hand, an east wind blows causing the waters to recede on either side of the people of Israel.

23. When the Egyptians try to pursue them, it is too dark.

24. In the morning, God appears to the Egyptians in a pillar of fire and a cloud and throws the Egyptian army into confusion.

25. Their chariot wheels are clogged with mud and they conclude that God is on the side of Israel.

26. God tells Moses to stretch out his hand over the sea so the waters would come back upon the Egyptians, their chariots and their horsemen.

27. Moses lifts up his hand, the wind dies down and the waters flood back. It engulfs the Egyptians as they try to flee.

28. It wipes out all of the Egyptians.

29. But the Israelites walk across on dry ground.

30. Thus Adonai, the Lord, saves the children of Israel.

31. The people are impressed and respect God and his servant, Moses.

Chapter 15

Moses and the children of Israel sing: "I will sing to Adonai for he has triumphed gloriously; the horse and the rider he has thrown into the sea.

2. "He is mighty and glorious, The Lord JEHOVAH has become our savior; he is our God and we will praise him; our father's God, and we will exalt him.

3. "The Lord is a mighty warrior: Adonai is his name.

4. "Pharaoh's chariots and his host he cast into the sea; his valiant men also are drowned in the Reed Sea.

5. "The depths have covered them; they sank to the bottom like stones.

6. "Your right hand, O Lord, has become glorious in power; your right hand, O Lord, has defeated your enemies.

7. "And in the greatness of your might you have overthrown them that hate you; you sent your wrath, and consumed them like stubble.

8. "With blast of your breath, the waters piled up, the floods stood up as if it were sheepskins; the waves gathered in heaps in the heart of the sea.

9. "The enemy said, 'I will pursue, I will overtake, I will divide the spoil my soul will devour them; I will draw my sword, my hand shall destroy them.'

10. "You did blow with your wind, the sea covered them, they sank as lead in the mighty waters.

11. "Who is like unto thee, O Lord, O power of cause and effect, glorious in wholeness, revered and praised, doing wonders?
12. "You lifted your right hand; the earth swallowed them.

13. "In your mercy, you have led your people and saved them; you have guided them in your strength and wholeness.

14. "The people heard and were fearful. Fear took over the people of Philistia.

15. "Then the princes of Edom were afraid, the mighty men of Moab seized them; all the inhabitants of Canaan were heartbroken.

16. "Fear and dread shall fall upon them. Your power sank them until your people passed over."

17. "You shall bring your people in and plant them on the mountain of your inheritance. Your people are lifted to a higher consciousness and duplicate your nature.

18. "Your nature shall rule forever.

19. "The Egyptians went into the sea. But the Israelites walked on dry land."

20. Miriam, prophetess and sister of Aaron takes the timbrel (tambourine) in her hand and leads all the women.

21. They sing and Miriam answers, "Sing to the Lord, for he has triumphed gloriously; the horse and rider he has thrown into the sea."

22. So Moses leads the people to the wilderness of Sur or Shud

15. Upon seeing the manna, the Israelites wonder, "What is it?" Moses replies, "This is the bread God gives you to eat."

16. Gather an omer for every man according to the number in his tent.

17. And they do, some more, some less.

18. Everyone has just he right amount to eat.

19. "Don't leave any for the next morning," Moses advises.

20. But some people don't follow his instruction and it rots and gathers worms and stinks. Moses gets angry with them.

21. They gather it daily and when the sun gets hot, it melts.

22. On the sixth day, they gather twice as much, two omers for every person. The elders come and tell Moses.

23. Moses explains, "This is what God has said, 'Tomorrow is a day of holy rest, a Sabbath to the Lord. Bake what you will bake today and cook what you will cook, and keep that which is left over cold for yourselves until morning.

24. So they keep some of it cold for the next day and it did not rot or stink and there were not worms in it.

25. Moses says, "Eat today but do not gather in the fields for it is a Sabbath day to the Lord.

26. "Six days you shall gather it; but on the seventh day gather none."

27. When some try gathering manna on the seventh day, they don't find any.

28. God says to Moses, "How long will you folks refuse to follow my instructions?

29. "It's because of the Sabbath day that you are given two days of bread, so you don't need to even come out of your household to get food on the Sabbath."

30. So the people rest on the seventh day.

31. The bread is white coriander seed and tastes like honeycomb. They call it manna.

32. God tells Moses to fill a portion (an omer) full of manna to be kept for generations so they may see the bread God provided.

33. Moses and Aaron take an omer full of manna to save.

34. And Aaron sets it aside.

35. The children of Israel eat manna for the forty years that they journey until they reach the border of Canaan.

36. An Omer is one-tenth of an ephah (clearing of the mind).

Chapter 17.

Everyone of the Israelites travel from Seen to Rephidim (place of rest after victory) where there is no drinkable water.

2. They complain to Moses.

3. They are upset with him that he brought them out of Egypt only to face drought.

4. Moses prays.

5. God responds, guiding Moses to take some of the elders with him and the staff he had used at the river.

6. "I shall be with you as you stand before the flinty rock at Horeb and strike it so that water gushes forth and the people can drink."

7. Moses does as instructed and names the place Temptation, since the people had questioned God's presence and they must fight off negativity and doubts.

8. The Amalekites (lustfulness) attack.

9. Moses tells Joshua to choose men to go and fight Amelek tomorrow. "And I will stand on top of the hill with the staff of God in my hand."

10. So Joshua prepares for battle and Moses, Aaron and Hur (affirmative prayer) stand on top of the hill.

11. When Moses lifts up his arms the Israelites prevail,

12. But when Moses arms become tired and are lowered, Amelek prevails. So they place a stone where Moses can sit on it and Aaron and Hur support Moses arms, one on each side, and Moses' arms remain steady all day.

13. And Joshua defeats Amalek with the edge of his sword, cutting through the negativity.

14. God tells Moses to write about this in his journal in order to remember the event, as the Law of Cause and Effect will obliterate any memory of the influence of Amalek.

15. Moses builds an altar there naming it Jehovah-nasi, commemorating

God's victory over negativity.

16. And reconfirming spirituality's power for all time.

Chapter 18

His excellence, Jethro, priest of Midian who is Moses' father-in-law, hears of all that God has done for Moses and for the people of Israel, and that the Lord God has brought them out of Egypt.

2. Jethro brings Moses' wife, Zipporah, back to him as she had been staying with her father.

3. He also brings Moses' sons, Gershon (isolation following violence),

4. And Eliezer (God, my help).

5. Jethro comes with his sons and his wife to the encampment at the mountain of God (a place of high consciousness.)

6. Moses is told of this.

7. He goes out to meet them and they embrace and go into the tent.

8. Moses tells Jethro of all that has taken place.

9. Jethro rejoices for all that the Divine has done.

10. He says, "Blessed be Spirit that you have been delivered out of Egypt and out of the hands of Pharoah.

11. "God is so good."

12. Jethro makes burnt offerings and sacrifices to the Lord God joined by Aaron and all the elders. They celebrate.

13. The next day, Moses holds the high watch as people come to him with their challenges, disagreements and issues.

14. Jethro sees all that Moses does for the people from morning 'til night.

15. Moses explains what he does to Jethro.
16. But Jethro thinks Moses will burn himself out doing so much for everybody.

17 ."You'll wear yourself out; you can't do it alone.

18. "You must become a teacher from God to the people to bring their challenges before God.

19. "Show them how to use the Law for their highest benefit and to be God's instruments, doing good works.

20. "Furthermore, find strong men who have a high respect for God, who are truthful and have high integrity; and appoint them as leaders of thousands, hundreds, fifties and tens.

21. "Let them sit as counselors, working with peoples issues, challenges, differences and upsets. And when there is a problem too big for them to handle, then they can bring it to you.

22. "In this way, you'll be able to handle it and everyone will live in a consciousness of peace."

23. Moses listens to the advice of his father-in-law and does what Jethro tells him.

24. Moses chooses able men and appoints them as counselors and officers over the people; leaders of thousands, hundreds, fifties and

tens.

25. They take care of all the small matters and take the more difficult cases to Moses.

26. Then his father-in-law leaves and goes back to his own land.

Chapter 19

Three months after they leave Egypt, the people of Israel come to the wilderness of Seen also known as Sinai (an exalted or high place in consciousness in which there is a feeling of conscious communion with Spirit).

2. They camp before Mount Horeb or Sinai, where Moses had previously heard God's instructions to lead the children of Israel out of Egypt.

3. Moses ascends the mountain or raises his consciousness to such a high level that he hears Divine instructions again.

4. God points out how Moses and his followers have witnessed God's power and seen how this Love energy freed them from the Egyptians. "I bore you up as on eagles' wings and brought you to myself.

5. "As you listen to the spiritual voice within you and follow my Divine guidance, my Law returns only good to you.

6. "You are my kingdom, my priests and a holy people. Speak these words to the Children of Israel."

7. And Moses calls the elders together and communicates what Spirit had said.

8. Unanimously, the people agree.

9. God confirms that he appears in a thick cloud so that the people can hear him.

10. Spirit tells the people, through Moses, to wash their clothes, symbolizing a cleansed consciousness.

11. "In three days, I will appear on Mount Sinai," says God.
12. "Because the people believe they need to fear me, tell them not to come near the mountain or the law will return harm upon them since their belief is so powerful.

13. "So tell the people not to touch the mountain until after the trumpet goes silent."

14. Moses tells this to the people and the people wash their clothes.

15. He tells them to be ready on the third day and suggests they not touch their wives as that might distract them from purely spiritual thoughts.

16. And on the morning of the third day, it begins to thunder and there is lightning and a thick cloud appears on Mount Sinai. There is an exceedingly loud trumpet blast. The people tremble.

17. Moses leads the people to the base of the mountain.

18. The whole mountain is smoking and quakes gently.

19. The sound of the trumpet grows louder and louder and when Moses speaks, God answers with his voice.

20. God is standing at the top of the mountain and calls Moses to come to the top (raise his consciousness).

21. God tells Moses to warn the people not to gaze on God or they'll perish since that's what they believe.

22. Spirit says the priests who come near should purify their consciousness.

23. Moses points out that the people cannot come to the top of the mountain as God has warned.

24. The Lord God tells Moses to go down and bring Aaron back up with him, but no others.

25. So Moses does that.

Chapter 20

God says,

2. "I am the Lord your God, who brought you out of the land of Egypt (sense consciousness) into freedom and these are ten of your freedoms:

3. "You shall know that there is only one God (# I)

4. "You shall not need to make anything else your God (# II).

5. "Neither worshipping nor serving them

6. "Since I show love to those who love me.

7. "You can use my name (nature) for good (# III). You'll find great joy in seeing all that you can cause to be created.

8. "You can keep a Sabbath day holy (# IV). After you've been working hard, it feels good to relax.

9, "Labor for six days,

10. "Then take a day off.

11. "Using the original creation myth as your example.

12. "You are free to honor your parents (# V). It feels good to share close family ties and the love for one another that is naturally there.

13. "You are free to support life keeping others alive (# VI). No one wants to destroy anyway.

14. "You are free to be faithful enjoying mutual trust (# VII). It can be meaningful and joyful being in a relationship where you can totally trust each other in unconditional love.

15. "You shall enjoy all of my abundance with no need to take from others (# VIII). My infinite supply provides everyone with everything they need, want and desire.

16. "You are free to be honest, always telling the truth about your neighbor or anyone (# IX). It is freeing to withhold nothing.

17. "You are free to know with confidence that there's plenty for everyone in ample supply because I, your God, am infinitely generous (# X) There's just no need for the nagging feeling of jealousy."

18. The people observe the thunder and lightning, the sound of the trumpet and the smoking mountain and are highly impressed, but fearful, too.

19. The people are of the opinion that it is best for Moses to tell them what God says, rather than hearing it from God directly, because they believe they would die in that event.

20. Moses points out that the people can have a direct connection with Spirit.

21. Yet they keep their distance while Moses draws near God by sensing the Presence within.

22. God says, "I can talk to the people through the kingdom of heaven which is within them."

23. Spirit makes it clear that the people no longer need to make silver or gold images projecting a spiritual nature on them.

24. God indicates the earth is the only altar people need and it is the only place people need to make sacrifices. God will bless the people right where they are.

25. It is communicated that there's no need to use iron tools to make a stone altar.

26. Nor do you need to use steps to go up to the altar (God's altar is within you).

Chapter 21

These are judgments that God has given through intuitive guidance. They are rules which make the society of the Israelites work when followed.

2. Avoid keeping a person indebted to you endlessly. For example, when you employ someone, make the contract for six years, concluding with the seventh year.

3. At the end of the contract, each party leaves with what was theirs

when they entered into the agreement.

4. Giving another example, an unmarried man who enters into an agreement and subsequently accepts a wife from the other party, is not entitled to that wife and any children at the end of the contract.

5. An exception would be, if the husband and wife love each other, and he does not want to leave alone.

6. In this case, a person acting as judge may decree that the man remain under the contract in perpetuation if that is what all parties want.

7. If there is a rule about a man selling a daughter, until people awaken to the fact that people can't own other people, use common sense and fairness in all dealings.

8. A master can release a person with whom he is not pleased.

9. He should treat a daughter-in-law as he would his own daughter.

10. If he takes a second wife, he should be careful not to overextend himself so it doesn't take away from the first.

11. Otherwise, she is free to leave.

12. According to the law of cause and effect, if a man strikes another, he'll be stricken back.

13. But if he didn't hold evil intention behind his actions, the law will deal with him fairly. Love is more powerful than law.

14. Yet, if a man kills another treacherously, the law will deal with him accordingly.

15. Hitting a parent goes against life's natural order of authority.

16. Stealing or even owning another person creates negative consequences.

17. Cursing a parent ends up cursing the curser.

18. Whatever you do to another comes back upon you.

19. You are responsible for your actions.

20. Killing a person, even an employee, also comes back.

21. If he or she recovers, the consequences won't be as severe.

22. Hitting a woman with child has costly circumstances.

23. The law is always working.

24. It is very precise as in an eye for and eye, a tooth for a tooth, hand for hand, foot for foot.

25. Burning for burning, wound for wound, slap for slap. Even negative thoughts cause negative circumstances.

26. Free others who you've treated negatively, either physically or in consciousness.

27. You decide. It's up to you how you use the law.

28. Kill off the dangerous animalistic thoughts if you discover them within you.

29. The law holds one responsible who has not even previously dealt with negative aspects in consciousness.

30. There is a price to pay for unhealed negativity.

31. Accept responsibility.

32. You pay the price as part of the creative process.

33. If you have created a dangerous situation for others or for their property,

34. The real danger is the consequence you end up attracting to yourself through the law.

35. When you set things right, it reverses the consequences.

36. When you are fair, fairness comes back to you.

Chapter 22

Pay back what was not rightly yours, and the law gives pay back.

2. If you harm a person who is violating an agreement, you are not responsible for the harm.

3. He pays the price.

4. Double the price.

5. Restitution reverses the law.

6. A person who starts a fire suffers the consequences.

7. If a man causes harm to more than one other person, he has a double price to pay.

8. If you think about another person having a loss and they do, the law of cause and effect holds you accountable.

9. Restitution reverses the law.

10. If a man is blameless, the law forgives.

11. The innocent suffer no penalty.

12. But if a man fails to responsibly protect another's property, he is subjected to the law.

13. Divided thoughts reap divided results.

14. If you borrow an animal and it is injured or dies, you can replace it to make sure the same thing doesn't happen to your own.

15. But if the animal is injured or dies when the owner is present, the owner is responsible.

16. If desires manifest in physical out-picturing with a young woman, a man's marriage to her is required.

17. Agreed upon financial arrangements assure the highest outcome.

18. Do not allow misuse of the power of your subconscious.

19. Do not misuse sexual energy.

20. Do not make gods out of anything other than the Divine Spirit.

21. Embrace even those who are strangers. Everyone is spiritually connected.

22. Be good to those who could use your blessing, like widows and

orphans.

23. Remember, you experience the same energy you put out.

24. The blessing will return to you.

25. Avoid taking advantage of those who are already down and out.

26. If someone makes a pledge that would be harmful to them, forgive them and return what is rightfully theirs.

27. Be reasonable.

28. Support your leaders.

29. Be generous in giving back to the source of your spiritual nourishment.

30. Give in a timely manner.

31. Avoid ingesting contaminated ideas just as you would avoid meat that the wild animals have been eating.

Chapter 23

Have high integrity in keeping with your spiritual nature. Use the law beneficially following some practical guidelines:

2. Don't go along with mob mentality or negative race consciousness.

3. Don't side with the underdog just because you feel sorry for him.

4. If you find an animal belonging to your neighbor, return it.

5. Help an overburdened animal, even one belonging to an enemy.

6. Don't interfere with justice, even if you want to help a poor man.

7. Support the truth, the innocent and the righteous.

8. Don't accept bribes; be aligned with truth and integrity.

9. Be friendly and kind even to those who are different from yourself, even like you would have preferred to have been treated in Egypt.

10. Plant your land for six years, reaping the harvests.

11. The seventh year, leave it fallow, letting the less fortunate glean what is there. Leave the rest for wild animals.

12. That way the land is given a rest, even as you can work for six days and then rest on the seventh as in taking a Sabbath day, letting everyone get refreshed and renewed.

13. Remain focused on Spirit avoiding even thinking of false idols.

14. Three times a year, have a celebration.

15. Firstly, the feast of the unleavened bread, celebrating your freedom.

16. Secondly, celebrate the replanting the first fruits of your harvest. And thirdly, celebrate the ingathering of the crops at the end of the growing season.

17. Three times a year, show your gift offerings to recognize your abundance.

18. In these celebrations, remember that contaminated thinking is like mixing the blood of sacrificed animals with leavened bread or like

unhealthy practices such as leaving the sacrificed meat out all night. Clean your consciousness, clean your practices, and you'll have a clean life.

19. Bring the first fruits of your land into the house of the Lord your God. But don't contaminate your consciousness like considering cooking the meat of a kid in its own mother's milk.

20. You are guided and protected by God at all times. In fact, Spirit sends his messages via angelic messengers (intuition) to guide you to the promised land.

21. Listen to the intuitive messengers and do what they say.

22. If you follow them, God will protect you from enemies.

23. Spirit's angels will go before you and protect you from the Amorites, Hittites, Perizzites, Canaanites, Hivites and Jebusites. They'll be destroyed.

24. Don't worship their gods or follow their ways. You'll utterly overthrow them and break their statues.

25. Serve the Lord your God and Divine Wholeness will bless your bread and water and keep you healthy.

26. God says, "Nothing is against you and everything is for you. You will live a good, long life.

27. "Everywhere, your enemies will fear the power that is behind you and they'll flee from you.

28. "It will be like an invisible Force before you destroying the enemy armies.

29. "I won't destroy them in one year so the land won't become desolate and taken over by wild animals.

30. "Little by little, I'll destroy your enemies as you become stronger and stronger eventually taking over the land.

31. "Your boundaries will be from the Reed Sea as far a the sea of the Philistines, and from the desert to Euphrates River. And I will deliver the inhabitants of the land to you and you will overpower them.

32. "Make no agreements with them or their idols.

33. "They won't live in your land and you will not worship their gods so they won't be a stumbling block for you."

Chapter 24.

God says to Moses, "Come to me with Aaron, Nadab and Abihu (sons of Aaron who possess spiritual arrogance) and seventy elders of Israel. Worship a distance from me.

2. "Only Moses is to come near." Moses is the only one who has evolved his spiritual awareness to a high enough level to feel a close connection with Spirit.

3. Moses communicates all of the instructions about the law and about his spiritual connection and that he is to communicate what God says with Aaron, Nadab, Abihu and the seventy elders.

4. Moses writes the words God has told him, gets up early to build an altar at the foot of the mountain, and erects twelve pillars symbolizing the twelve tribes.

5. He has young men sacrifice oxen as peace offerings on the altar.

6. Moses takes half the blood from the oxen and pours it into basins, and sprinkles the other half on the altar.

7. He reads the covenant of freedoms that he has written down to the people, and everyone agrees to practice them.

8. Moses takes the blood and sprinkles it on the people, saying "This is the blood of the covenant of freedoms."

9. Then Moses, Aaron, Nadab, Abihu and the seventy elders go up the side of the mountain (raise their consciousness).

10. They see the God of Israel; under his feet is sapphire stone, clear as the sky.

11. They experience no harm. They eat and drink.

12. The Lord God tells Moses to come to the top of the mountain and "I will give you stone tablets on which I have written the freedoms."

13. Moses and Joshua rise up. Moses goes to the top of the mountain.

14. Moses tells the elders to wait for him to return. Aaron and Hur remain with the elders in case anyone has any problems.

15. Moses goes up the mountain and the top of it is covered with a cloud.

16. The cloud covers the top of the mountain for six days, and on the seventh day, God summons Moses into the midst of the cloud.

17. In the sight of all the children of Israel, Moses sees the glory of the Lord God appearing as a burning fire on top of the mountain.

18. Moses is there forty days and forty nights (full completion).

Chapter 25

Divine Intuition speaks to Moses. Saying,

2. "Communicate to the people of Israel a way to keep the channels of connection open between them and me via a free will offering. For everyone who gives willingly with his heart, receives offerings.

3. "Accept gold, silver and brass,

4. "Blue, purple and scarlet, fine linen and goats' hair,

5. "Rams' skins dyed red, skins dyed with vermilion, and acacia wood.

6. "Oil for lamps, spices for anointing oil, and for sweet incense,

7. "Onyx stones and precious stones to be set in the ephod (breastplate on a priest's garment representing spiritual understanding).

8. "Tell them to make a sanctuary where they can commune with their own spiritual nature.

9. "Follow the pattern I'll provide.

10. "Have them make an ark of Acacia wood to symbolically contain the spark of divinity within everyone. The dimensions shall be fifty inches long or two and a half cubits (a cubit is the length of a forearm from the tip of the middle finger to the elbow, an average of about 20 inches) and 1.5 cubits wide (30 inches) and 1.5 cubits (30 inches) high.

11. "Tell them to overlay the ark with the preciousness and purity of

gold.

12. "Make four rings to place at each corner

13. "And make two poles of acacia wood , overlaid with gold, about fifty inches long.

14. "Put the poles into the rings to carry the ark.

15. "The poles are permanently kept in the rings.

16. "Keep a copy of my agreements or covenants with you inside the ark.

17. "Make a mercy seat of pure gold about 50 inches long and 30 inches wide.

18. "Make two cherubim for each side of the mercy seat out of gold, the seat of the presence of the Divine.

19. "Place one cherub on each side of the mercy seat.

20. "Facing each other with their wings stretching upward to cover the seat.

21. "Place the mercy seat on top of the ark and inside the ark, place a copy of the agreement or covenant I will give you.

22. "I will meet you above the mercy seat between the two cherubim. Here you'll feel a divine connection.

23. "Also make a table out of acacia wood 40 inches long by 20 inches wide and about 30 inches high.

24. "Overlay it with pure gold and make a crown of gold for it

25 "And make a border out of gold, a hand's breadth wide (five inches).

26. "Make four rings of gold to be placed at each corner on the feet of the table.

27. "Place the rings near the border to insert poles through the rings to carry it.

28. "Make the poles out of acacia wood, overlay them with gold.

29. "Make dishes, spoons, jars and bowls made out of gold to serve wine.

30. "On the table, set shewbread (unleavened bread symbolizing all sustenance is of God.}

31. "Make a candlestick cast of one piece of gold including the shaft, branches, bowls, buds and floral decorations.

32. "Three branches shall come out of each side representing the Spirit, Soul and Body of the creative process.

33. "Three bowls shall appear to be fastened to each shaft with buds and flowers.

34. "On each candlestick, there shall be four bowls made to look like almonds with buds and flowers.

35. "There shall be a bud under each set of two branches.

36. "The buds and branches shall be made of one piece. All of it one piece indicating the oneness of the Spirit.

37. "Make seven lamps to give light, the light of God.

38. "And make snuffers and snuff dishes also out of pure gold.

39. "Use a talent (equivalent to thousands) to make all these vessels (containers of spiritual energy).

40. "Use the patterns and instructions I have given you from a higher consciousness.

Chapter 26

"Make a tabernacle with ten curtains of fine twined linen of blue (peaceful), purple (spiritual) and scarlet (love) material using fine workmanship and decorated with cherubim .

2. "The length of each curtain shall be 28 cubits (approximately 46 feet) and the breadth four cubits (approximately six and a half feet). Each curtain shall be the same size.

3. "Five curtains shall be connected and the other five coupled with each other.

4. "Make loops with blue on the edge of one curtain to the selvedged (finished off edging) to the edging on another curtain with loops on both edges.

5. "Each curtain shall have 50 loops lined up opposite each other.

6. "Make 50 taches (fasteners) of gold and couple the curtains together so it shall be one tabernacle.

7. "Make a roof out of goats hair composed of eleven sections with a length of thirty cubits (about 50 feet) and width of four cubits (around six and a half feet)

8. "The length of each section shall be 30 cubits (about 50 feet) and the breadth four cubits (approximately six and one-half feet).

9. "You shall couple five curtains by themselves and six curtains by themselves. Double the sixth curtain and place it in the front of the tabernacle.

10. "Make fifty loops on the edge of the curtain that is outermost coupling and fifty loops on the edge of the curtain which couples the second.

11. "Make fifty taches (fasteners) of brass and put the taches into the loops and couple the tent together making one tabernacle.

12. "What is left over of the curtains of the tent, the half curtain that remains, , shall hang over the back of the tabernacle.

13. "One cubit of the curtain shall hang over each side.

14. "Make a covering for the tent of rams' skins dyed red and a covering of rams' skins dyed vermilion. The Ram represents my strength.

15. "Make boards for the tabernacle of acacia wood, bringing life from trees into the tabernacle.

16. "The length of each board shall be ten cubits (about sixteen and a half feet) and the breadth one cubit and a half (about 30 inches).

17. "There shall be tenons (joints) at each end of each board to link them together indicating you are linked with me.

18. "Make twenty boards for the south side of the tabernacle.

19. "Make forty sockets of silver under the twenty boards, two sockets under one board for its two tenons and two sockets under another

board for its two tenons.

20. "And for the other side of the tabernacle, the north side of the tabernacle, there shall be twenty boards.

21. "And their forty sockets of silver; two sockets under one board and two sockets under another board.

22. "For the sides of the tabernacle, for the west side, you shall make six boards.

23. "Make two boards for two corners.

24. "They shall be even at the bottom and coupled together at the head of it to one ring. It shall be for both sockets. These shall be for two corners.

25. "There shall be eight boards, and their sockets of silver, symbolizing the shining light of my Spirit, sixteen (double infinity) sockets; two sockets under one board and two sockets under another board.

26. "Make bars of acacia wood; five for the boards of the one side of the tabernacle.

27. "And five bars for the boards for the other side of the tabernacle, at the westward side of the tabernacle.

28. "And the middle bar amid the boards shall reach from end to end.

29. "Make the bars of acacia wood and make rings of gold to hold the bars and overlay the bars with gold (purity).

30. "Build the tabernacle according to this pattern given to you out of a higher consciousness.

31. "Make a veil of blue (peaceful), purple (spiritual) and scarlet (love) material, and fine twined linen with cherubim depicting messengers from God.

32. "Hang the veil from four pillars made of acacia wood overlaid with gold; with hooks of gold upon four sockets of silver.

33. "Hang the veil under the taches (fasteners) and place the ark of the covenant in the most holy place and spread the veil between the holy place and most holy.

34. "Place the mercy seat upon the ark of the covenant in the most holy place.

35. "Set the table outside the veil with the candlestick opposite the table on the side of the tabernacle toward the south; and put the table on the north side.

36. "Make a curtain for the door of the tent of blue, purple and scarlet material with fine twined linen made of embroidered work.

37. "Hang the curtain from five pillars of acacia wood overlaid with gold with hooks made of gold and five sockets of brass.

Chapter 27

"Make an altar out of acacia wood, five cubits (about eight feet) and five cubits wide. So it is foursquare (balanced) and three cubits high (about five feet).

2. "Place horns made of the same material overlaid with brass on the four corners.

3. "Make pots and cauldrons with shovels and hooks and tongs and

censers (incense burners) to use on the altar. Make all the vessels and utensils of brass.

4. "Make a grating for the altar, a network of brass, with four rings of brass at the four corners.

5. "Put the grating under the ledge of the altar so the grate can reach to the middle of the altar.

6. "Make poles of acacia wood and overlay them with brass.

7. "Put the poles into the rings so that they are on both sides of the altar when carrying it.

8. "The table shall be hollow inside the boards.

9. "Make the court of the tabernacle on the south side with fine twined linen hangings 100 cubits long (around 160 feet)

10. "On twenty pillars with twenty brass sockets. The hooks and fillets (raised ridges on the column shall be silver.

11. "Also, the north side of the tabernacle shall have the hangings of the same length and pillars the same as the south side.

12. "For the breadth of the court on the west side, there shall be fifty cubit hangings (about 80 feet long) with ten pillars and ten sockets.

13. "And the width of the court on the east side shall be fifty cubits (about 80 feet).

14. "The hangings for one side of the gate of the court shall be fifteen cubits (about 24 feet) with three pillars and three sockets

15. "And on the other side there shall be 15 hangings and three pillars

and three sockets.

16." For the gate of the court, there shall be a hanging of 20 cubits (about 32 feet) of blue and purple and scarlet material of fine twined linen with embroidered work hung on four pillars with four sockets.

17. "All the pillars around the court shall be filleted with silver, and the sockets with brass.

18. "The length of the court shall be 100 cubits (about 160 feet) and the width 50 cubits (about 80 feet) and the height five cubits (about 8 feet) with fine twined linen and their sockets.

19. "All the vessels and pins of the tabernacle and all the tent–pins of the court shall be brass.

20. "Instruct the people of Israel to bring you pure olive oil from beaten olives for the light, so that the lamps may burn continuously.

21. "Every evening to morning, have Aaron and his sons light the lamps which are to be placed outside the veil next to the ark containing the covenant, according to my instructions.

Chapter 28

"Bring Aaron (Spiritual strength) and his sons Nadab (Presumptuous use of spiritual thoughts), Abihu (Divine sonship) , Eleazar (Spiritual strength), and Ithamar (Victorious state of consciousness) to you from among the children of Israel to serve in the capacity of priests.

2. "Make holy vestments for Aaron to honor his priestly position with glory and beauty.

3. "Speak to everyone who I have filled with the Spirit of wisdom so they

may make the holy vestments for Aaron to consecrate him as head priest serving as my minister.

4. "Have those with a wisdom consciousness include a breastplate, an richly embroidered ephod, a robe, an embroidered coat, a mitre for his head and a girdle encircling as the holy vestments for Aaron and his sons.

5. "Have them use gold (abundance), blue (peaceful), purple (spiritual) and scarlet (love) material and fine twined linen as woven by a craftsman.

6. "Use material of the same colors and the fine linen for the ephod.

7. "It shall have the shoulder pieces joined at the two edges.

8. "The embroidered girdle of the ephod shall be made of the same material and colors.

9. "Use two onyx stones and engrave the names of the sons of Israel on them;

10. "Six on one stone and six on the other, listed according to the order of their birth.

11. "The stones bearing the twelve names shall be mounted on settings of gold.

12. "Place the two stones upon the shoulders of the ephod as a memorial of the sons of Israel.

13. "Make settings of gold.

14. "And two braided chains of pure gold which are connected to the settings.

15. "The breastplate of discernment shall be made of gold and material of blue (peace), purple (spiritual), and scarlet (love) and fine twined linen.

16. "It shall be foursquare (balance), a span (about nine inches) in each direction.

17. "Place settings of stones in the breastplate in four rows. The first row shall have sardius (a precious red stone indicating protection and strength), topaz (crystal providing peace), and emerald (clarity of thinking).

18. "In the second row place carbuncle or garnet (natural energy and protection), a sapphire (purity, serenity, beauty and love) jasper (calmness and grace).

19. "In the third row, place Jacinth also known as zircon (beauty, love and peace), carnelian (healing), and an amethyst (serenity and spirituality).

20. "In the fourth row, place a beryl (peace), onyx (protection) and jasper (calmness and grace).

21. "The stones shall be engraved with the names of the twelve sons of Israel.

22. "And you shall two chains made of pure gold.

23. "And make two rings of pure gold on the breastplate and put the two rings on the two ends of the breastplate.

24. "Fasten the two braided chains of gold on the two rings which are on the ends of the breastplate.

25. "And the other two ends of the braided chains are to be fastened to the two setting and put on the shoulder pieces of the ephod in front of it.

26. "And make two rings of gold and place them on the two ends of the breastplate on the border of the ephod.

27. "Make two rings of gold and put them on the two shoulder pieces of the ephod underneath toward the front above the embroidered girdle.

28. "Bind the breastplate by its rings to the rings of the ephod with a blue lace so it will rest upon the embroidered girdle of the ephod, and the breastplate won't come loose from the ephod.

29. "Aaron shall wear the names of the sons of Israel in the breastplate of discernment upon his heart, when he enters the holy place as a memorial.

30. "And you shall put in the breastplate of discernment the Urim (light) and thummin (truth) and they'll be on Aaron's heart when he enters into the Presence of Spirit.

31. "Make the robe of the ephod blue (peace).

32. "Make an opening in the middle of top of the robe with a hemmed, woven binding so it won't tear.

33. "Decorate the hem of the robe with pomegranates symbolizing fruitfulness with bells of gold interspersed between each pomegranate, which shall be blue, purple and scarlet.

34. "So, there's a golden bell, a pomegranate, a bell, a pomegranate all around the opening on the hem of the robe.

35. "Aaron shall wear the robe as a protective garment as he enters the holy place to minister and the sounds of the bells on the robe are heard as he goes in and leaves.

36. "Make a crown of pure gold and engrave the words HOLINESS TO THE LORD GOD on it.

37. "Put it on blue lace so it may be upon the front of the mitre.

38. "Aaron shall wear it, representing the God nature within every person, the crowning glory that is the Holy Spirit expressing. The Aaron consciousness within everyone vibrates at a higher level absorbing lesser thoughts and actions and dissolving them into the nothingness that they are. As Aaron sacrifices the belief in separation, it is replaced by that Divine nature of Love and Light.

39. "Make the coat and the mitre of fine linen and the girdle of embroidered work reflecting the Divine role Aaron wears.

40. For Aaron's sons, make coats and girdles and bonnets all symbolizing the Aaron (spiritual) nature within them.

41. "Place all of these symbols of Divinity upon Aaron and his sons recognizing their heightened consciousness.

42. "Also make knee length trousers for them to wear.

43. "They shall wear all these garments when they enter the tabernacle and when they come near to the altar.

Chapter 29

"As a symbolic sacred consecration of Aaron and his sons, perform the following ceremony. Begin with a young bull and two rams that are without blemishes. The priest will be sacrificing his animal nature to focus on the spiritual energy.

2. "Using unleavened bread (a reminder of the freedom inherited from previous generations) and oil symbolizing the light within, make a fine wheat flour.

3. "Put them in a basket and bring them and the bullock and rams to the door of the tabernacle.

4. "Bring Aaron and his sons to the door also. And wash them with water symbolizing a cleansed consciousness.

5. "Then place the vestments upon Aaron including the coat, robe, breastplate, the embroidered girdle and ephod.

6. "Place the mitre on his head and the holy crown on the mitre.

7. "Take the anointing oil, pouring it on his head to anoint him. Because the oil is also used to create light in the lamps, it symbolizes the Light within Aaron.

8. "Bring the sons and put coats upon them.

9. "Surround them with the girdles as they are surrounded with Light. Place bonnets on them recognizing Divine intelligence guiding their way.

10. Bring the young bull to the tabernacle and have Aaron and his sons place their hands upon its' head.

11. "Slaughter the bull there at the door of the tabernacle.

12. "Sprinkle some of the blood of the bull on the horns of the altar with your fingers and pour the rest at the bottom of the altar.

13. "Burn the entrails on the altar.

14. "But burn the flesh, skin and dung outside the camp [probably for sanitary purposes].

15. "Aaron and his sons shall take one ram (animal strength) and place their hands upon its head as a gesture of blessing the ram.

16. "Slaughter the ram (gain power)

17. "Cut pieces, wash them and put them over its head.

18. "Burn the whole ram upon the altar as a burnt offering to the Lord God, symbolizing the giving of the best in life to Spirit.

19. "Take the other ram and have Aaron and his sons place their hands upon its head.

20. "Slaughter this ram, too. Take some blood and sprinkle it on the tip Aaron's right ear and on the tips of the right ears of his sons and on the thumbs of their right hands and big toes of their right feet (encompassing the whole being) and upon the altar.

21. "Take some of the blood and some of the anointing oil and sprinkle it upon Aaron and his vestments and upon his sons and their vestments, so they are consecrated (dedicated to Spirit).

22. "Take the fat and the rump and the fat of internal organs and the right shoulder as it is a calf of consecration.

23. "Take one loaf of bread and a loaf of baked bread and a cake baked with flour and oil out of the basket of unleavened bread that is placed before God.

24. "Put all of these in the hands of Aaron and his sons and use a wave

motion presenting them to God.

25. "And they shall hand them out as they burn the breast of the ram upon the altar so the sweet savor adds to the sense of well-being and recognition of the Divine nature in all life.

26. "Take the breast of the ram that is Aaron's consecration making a wave motion as a presentation to God. Each will have a share, showing that the spiritual nature is within all.

27. "Dedicate the breast and the thigh placing them on the altar.

28. "It is like a peace offering recognizing the spiritual nature in Aaron an his sons and the giving nature of the children of Israel.

29. "The holy vestments of Aaron shall belong to his sons after him, to be consecrated for them as well.

30. "And one of his sons, who is to designated as priest in place of Aaron shall put the vestments on for seven days when he enters the tabernacle to minister in this holy place.

31. "And to cook the meat of the ram of holy consecration.

32. "Aaron and his sons shall eat of the meat of the ram and the bread that is in the basket at the door of the tabernacle of the congregation; all of this to indicate they have integrated the nature of Spirit into their consciousness.

33. "They shall eat of these things showing at-one-ment, but a stranger shall not eat them as they are holy.

34. "And any that is left over shall be burned the next morning.

35. "Consecrate Aaron and his sons in this way for seven days until the

ceremony is complete.

36. "Each of those days, offer a young bull, anointing it at the altar.

37. "The altar shall be holy and those touching it shall be holy (expressing the wholeness within them).

38. "Offer two lambs (the substance of life), each one year old, on the altar daily;

39. "One in the morning and the other in the evening (encompassing the entire day).

40. "With one lamb, offer one tenth of a portion of fine flour mixed with a fourth (balanced) part of a bottle of oil and a fourth of a bottle of wine for symbolically drinking in Spirit.

41. "Offer the other lamb in the evening, prepared by fire to represent the fire of Spiit.

42. "Do this throughout the generations at the door of the tabernacle where I reveal my unity with all.

43. "There I will meet the children of Israel,

44. "And sanctify the tabernacle and Aaron and his sons to lift their consciousness to the level of Divinity.

45. "And I will dwell within and among the children of Israel and I will be their God."

Chapter 30

"Make an altar of acacia wood to burn incense upon;

2. "Make it square, a cubit on each side (about 20 inches) and two cubits high with horns of the same material.

3. "Overlay it with pure gold.

4. "Under the crown of on the two corners, make two golden rings for the poles to carry the altar.

5. "Make the poles of acacia wood, overlaid with gold.

6. "Place it before the veil which is by the ark of the covenant. I will be present there.

7. "Aaron shall burn sweet incense every morning.

8. "When he lights the lamps in the evening, he shall perpetually burn incense symbolizing the continual presence of God.

9. "Don't use the incense altar for other purposes like burnt offerings or drink offerings.

10. "Aaron shall do a ceremony of at-one-ment using the horn of it once a year throughout the generations."

11. Presence of the Lord God speaks to Moses saying,

12. "When you count the people, every man shall give of himself so that out of a consciousness of generosity, his mind is open to receive God's blessings including perfect wholeness.

13. "When counted, each shall give half a shekel as a love offering.

14. "Everyone at least twenty years of age shall give the offering.

15. "The rich shall not give more, and the poor shall not give less than half a shekel as a way to feel at-one-ment with Spirit.

16. "Give the money to the work of the tabernacle."

17. God speaks to Moses, saying,

18. "Make a lavatory of brass placed between the tabernacle of the congregation and the altar. Place water in it.

19. "Aaron and his sons shall wash their hands and feet there representing the cleansing of consciousness.

20. "When they enter the tabernacle, they shall wash with water elevating their consciousness to a higher level of expressing life.

21. "And sealing their agreement for generations."

22. Further, Spirit speaks to Moses saying,

23. "Take the choicest spices, 500 units of myrrh (a gummy resin), 250 units of sweet cinnamon (spicy smelling)

24. "And 250 units of sweet calamus (a legume or root) and mix this incense symbolizing the Creative Process with a gallon and a half of olive oil (inferring the presence of light)

25. "Making a holy anointing oil.

26. "And anoint the tabernacle with it as well as the ark of the covenant,

27. "And the table and all its vessels, and the candlestick and its vessels, and the altar of incense,

28. "And the altar of the burnt offering with all its vessels, and the

lavatory and its base.

29. "Sanctify them, making them most holy; whoever touches them shall be holy.

30. "Anoint Aaron and his sons, consecrating them to serve.

31. "Speak to the children of Israel saying, 'This shall be a holy anointing oil recognizing the Divine Presence throughout the generations.

32. "'It shall not be rubbed on men's bodies like any other oil because it is a holy anointing oil.

33. "'Whomever makes it for others or gives any of it to a stranger shall feel cut off from their spirituality as it shall be holy to you'."

34. And God says to Moses, "Take an equal portion of three sweet spices, with pure frankincense,

35. "A pure and holy perfume,

36. "Beat some of it very fine and place it before the covenant where I am present with you; it is very holy.

37. "Make it for God, not for yourself.

38. "Those using it selfishly shall be cut off from spirituality."

Chapter 31

The Lord God speaks to Moses, saying,

2. "I have called the nature of Bezaliel (Divine sonship), son of Uri (enlightened), son of Hur (brilliant) of the tribe of Judah (praise Spirit).

3. " I have filled him with the Spirit of God, in wisdom and in understanding, and in knowledge and in all manner of workmanship.

4. "To do cunning works; in gold, silver and brass,

5. "And in the art of cutting stones to be set, and in the carving of timber and in all manner of workmanship.

6. "I have also appointed Elihab, son of Alisamach (supportive) son of Dan (judgement). And I have put wisdom in the hearts of every skillful man that they may make all things I have commanded you:

7. "Including the tabernacle of the congregation, the ark of the covenant, the mercy seat and all the vessels of the tabernacle,

8. "And the table and all its vessels and the pure candlestick with all its instruments, and the altar of incense,

9. "And the altar of burnt offering with all its vessels and the lavatory and its base,

10. "And the vestments for the service, and the holy vestments for Aaron the priest, and the vestments for his sons to serve the people on my behalf,

11. "And the anointing oil and sweet incense for the Holy places; according to all I have commanded you."

12. And God speaks to Moses, saying,

13. "Speak to the children of Israel saying, 'You must keep my Holy days as a sign between us throughout your generations that you may know that I am the Lord your God, who sanctifies (raises your level of spiritual consciousness).

14. "'Keep the Sabbath throughout the years as a perpetual agreement.

15. "'Work for six days, but rest on the seventh, so you'll sustain your aliveness.'

16. "The Children of Israel shall keep the Sabbath, observing it perpetually.

17. "It is a sign between us as a reminder that God made the heaven and the earth and the seas and all that are in it in six days and on the seventh (symbolizing completion), God rested."

18. And in concluding speaking to Moses on the mountain (when Moses' consciousness is high, God gives Moses two tablets of agreement written by the Divine nature.

Chapter 32

When it is taking a long time for Moses to come back down from the mountain, the people meet together with Aaron requesting that he make them gods so they can go up the mountain, because they don't know what has become of Moses.

2. "Remove the gold earrings from your wives and children and bring them to me."

3. So the people bring the gold jewelry to Aaron,

4. And he receives it all and draws a design and makes a molten calf. They say, "This is our God, O Israel, who brought us up out of the Egypt consciousness."

5. Aaron is fearful and builds an altar before the molten calf

proclaiming, "Tomorrow is a feast to God."

6. They arise early the next day and offer peace offerings, and the people sit down to eat and drink and stand to get rowdy.

7. Moses receives the intuitive message from Spirit within to go away from the mountain top as "your people have corrupted themselves."

8. "They have turned away from what I commanded and have made a molten calf and have worshipped it and sacrificed to it and said it is the God that brought them out of Egypt."

9. And God says to Moses, "I have seen these people and they are a stiff necked people (extremely stubborn).

10. "So, My Law of Cause and Effect will destroy them, but I will make a great nation of your descendants."

11. But Moses prays saying, "Don't let the Law destroy them after going to all the trouble to free them from a negative, outer focused life.

12. "The Egyptians will think Spirit brought them out of their land, only to destroy them." He argues for reconciliation.

13. Moses reminds himself and states it, as if God could possibly have any memory challenges: "Remember the promises you made to our ancestors that you would multiply their descendents and they would inherit the land for ever."

14. His argument works and the destructive direction of the Law is reversed.

15. Moses goes down the mountain with the two stone tablets representing Divine ideas,

16. These are God's statements written on both sides of the tablets (looking from all viewpoints0, that seem carved in stone.

17. As they approach the camp, Joshua notices the noise of the crowd fighting and says it seems to be the sound of war.

18. Moses, coming out of his spiritually enlightened state of mind, observes that it is not the sound of mighty or weak men, but of people focusing on an outer world, materialistic point of view. It's the sound of separation from the Divine.

19. When Moses sees the golden calf and hears the cymbals, he loses his temper and throws the tablets to the ground, shattering them.

20. Moses melts the calf in the fire, then takes the dust and sprinkles it on the drinking water, requiring everyone to drink it.

21. Moses criticizes Aaron for leading the people astray, so that they would act this way.

22. Aaron responds, "Don't be angry. You know how bad these people are.

23. "They wanted me to make gods for them because they didn't know what had become of you, their leader.

24. "And I told them to bring gold to me and I melted it into the form of a calf."

25. When Moses realizes that the people had been mistaken and that Aaron misled them.

26. He stands at the front of the camp and encourages them to rethink and to recommit themselves to their spiritual nature, which the Levites are the first to do.

27. He orders them to take their swords, cutting through the false thinking and let everyone make the decision to choose the spiritual path; the path of life rather than the path of death.

28. Some three thousand men chose death, the creative process multiplied to cause the effects of self destruction.

29. Moses acknowledges the strength of the Levites because of their total commitment to the path of Life. He says they were to receive a blessing.

30. The next day, Moses tells the people that he will raise his consciousness by going up the mountain again. In this heightened state of mind, he will sense the forgiving nature of God.

31. So, Moses returns to the mountain acknowledging what the people have done and receiving the awareness that Spirit always forgives since God is love.

32. So, Moses aligns with a consciousness of love and forgiveness. He wants so much for the people to be forgiven that he is even willing to let his own identity be obliterated for their sake.

33. God tells Moses, "People are responsible for their own actions. I am not even real to those who maintain an identity of separation from me, and without a relationship with me, there is no spiritual direction in their lives.

34. "Therefore now go, lead the people to the place where I tell you; Divine guidance shall go before you. Everyone chooses their own destiny and they receive the results accordingly.

35."The Law of Cause and Effect results in negative results when the people mistake the golden calf for Spirit within."

Chapter 33

Divine Spirit tells Moses to depart and go to the land (consciousness) he promised Abraham, Isaac and Jacob "and which I will give to your descendents.

2. "My Divine Intelligence shall guide you and make the way easy as the Canaanites (materialistic), Amorites (haughtiness), Hittites (resistance), Perizzites (scattered; unfocused), Hivites (physical) and the Jebusites (contention) practically vacate the land before you.

3. "Go to a land flowing with milk and honey (and abundance of nourishment and sweetness). But when you act like stiff necked people (stubbornly shutting out your spiritual nature}, the journey is tedious and sucks your energy."

4. The people are saddened by this message. They open their hearts and let their vulnerability show.

5. The Lord God says to Moses. "Tell the people that even in their stubborn state of mind, my nature will come upon them in an instant, moving beyond their armor revealing their true Divine nature. I will know them.

6. And the children of Israel let down their guard by mount Horeb, where the presence of God feels very real.

7. Moses takes his tent outside the camp, away from any negativity and limited consciousness and calls it the tabernacle of the congregation. And everyone who wants to commune with Spirit goes there.

8. Whenever Moses goes out to the tabernacle, all the people stand in the doorways of their tents and watch him until he enters the tabernacle.

9. When Moses enters the tabernacle, the pillar of cloud descends and stands at the door of the tabernacle and talks with Moses.

10. And as the people see the pillar of cloud standing at the door of the tabernacle, they rise up (their very consciousness is lifted).

11. The Lord God speaks to Moses face to face as a man speaks to a friend. Then he returns to the camp. But his servant, Joshua, stays in the tabernacle.

12. Moses says to God, "You tell me to bring up these people, but you haven't told me who you'll send with me, even though you've said, "I know your nature and you have found favor with me."

13. "Now if that is so, show me how I may know You and how it is that you see us as a great nation."

14. God tells Moses, "Go before me and I will give you rest."

15. Moses suggests, "If you yourself won't go with us, why not just let us stay here?

16. "How can anyone tell that we have found mercy in your sight? Wouldn't it be better if you went with us so that we could be distinguished from all the other people of the earth?

17. Finally, the Lord God responds, "I will do what you ask because I find you worthy of grace. I know your inner nature."

18. Moses wants to see the amazing glory of God.

19. Divine Spirit says "All of my goodness will be made apparent and I will be gracious and merciful to those who let grace and mercy be revealed to them.

20. "But you cannot see my face (the totality of my being) because you can't possibly take it all in. As long as you are living in a physical body, the experience of being all of Spirit will elude you. You can't see me and live in the form you are living.

21. "Imagine a rock in front of me on which you stand and feel my presence as I pass by, but you don't see my face even though you feel my hand upon you.

22. "After I pass, you will see my back but not my face. So, in retrospect you can be aware of the effect I will have had.

23. Looking back, you can realize all I do, but my face shall not be seen."

Chapter 34

The Lord God says to Moses, "Make two tablets of stone like the first ones; and write upon the tablet the Ten Freedoms that were on the first tablets that you broke.

2. "And in the morning come up to the top of mount Sinai and present yourself to me (raise your consciousness).

3. "Don't bring anyone else with you or let them even be on the mountain. And don't let your flocks or herds graze nearby. We'll meet one-on-one without distractions."

4. Moses hews two tablets of stone like the first and rises early in the morning and goes to the top of mount Sinai as he was told. He takes the

stone tablets with him.

5. The Lord God descends in the cloud and stands with Moses revealing the Divine nature.

6. God passes by him proclaiming "I am love, abundance, goodness and truth.

7. "I am merciful, forgiving, yet providing the effects of the causes entered into the law of mind. I perpetuate love and law for generations upon generations to the third and fourth generation."

8. Moses immediately lays down on the ground worshipping the Presence of the most High.

9. He prays, "If I have found mercy in your eyes, join me and my people in our journey, even though we have been stubborn. In your forgiveness, we let go of guilt."

10. God answers, "I will make a covenant with all your people: I will do marvels never before seen on earth showing my all-powerful nature.

11. "Observe my instructions and I will remove all limitations such as the Canaanites (materialism), Amorites (haughtiness), Hittites (resistance), Perizzites (scattered; unfocused), Hivites (physical) and the Jebusites (contention).

12. "Be cautious that you don't make any agreements with these lower energies, so you can avoid stumbling blocks.

13. "In fact, destroy their altars and representations of a false nature.

14. "Worship no other gods for I am a zealous God.

15. "Don't make a covenant with the inhabitants of the land, to avoid

the people going astray.

16. "Intermarry but be careful that your children avoid adopting their religious views.

17. Make yourselves no molten (symbols of erroneous) gods.

18. "Keep the feast of unleavened bread (Passover) in the month of Abib, the time that you came out of Egypt.

19. "Dedicate all the first born to me; your cattle, oxen and lambs. (In other words, acknowledge I am the source of all life).

20. "Exchange the first born of your cattle with a lamb. Value peace of mind more than riches. And value your first born son so much that you give him an awareness of his God-like nature, informing him of how loved he is.

21. "Work six days and rest on the seventh.

22. "Observe the feast of weeks taking the time to celebrate the passing of time. Observe the feast of the first fruits, an opportunity to put God first.

23. "Bring your love offerings to Spirit three times a year celebrating the Creative Process that blesses your life.

24. "I will provide ease and joy as you inherit your land and its abundance.

25. "Don't mix sacred ceremony with an outer worldly focus."

26. God communicates to give the first fruits to Spirit and respect the holiness involved in the preciseness of Sacred sacrifice.

27. God tells Moses to make a written documentation of his words and the covenant he is making with his people.

28. Moses connects with Spirit for forty days and forty nights, that is, until completion. He remains so focused that he goes without bread or water. He writes the Ten Freedoms on the tablets.

29. When Moses comes down from Mount Sinai, his face shines with spiritual radiance.

30. When Aaron and all the children of Israel see face glowing, they are afraid to come close.

31. So, Moses calls to them and Aaron and all the leaders return to him.

32. Eventually, all the children of Israel come near and Moses tells them all that God had communicated.

33. When Moses finishes speaking with them, he covers his face with a veil.

34. And when Moses goes in the tabernacle to talk to God, he removes the veil until he comes out and once again speaks of all God has commanded.

35. The children of Israel observe Moses' face shining.

Chapter 35

Moses gathers all the congregation together and reviews all that God has told him.

2. "Work for six days and take the seventh day off. A violation of this commandment lessens the experience of a fullness of life.

3. "Don't even build a fire on the Sabbath.

4. Moses says, "This is what God commands:

5. "Take a love offering for Spirit. Let whomever has an open heart bring gold, silver and brass,

6. "Blue, purple and scarlet materials, fine linen and goats hair,

7. "And rams' skins dyed red, and dark blue skins, and acacia wood.

8. "And oil for the light and spices for anointing oil and for the sweet incense.

9. "And bring onyx stones and precious stones for the ephod, and for the breastplate.

10. "Let every wise-hearted one among you come and make all the Lord instructed that we make:

11. "The tabernacle, tent, covering, taches, boards, bars, pillars and sockets,

12. "The ark, poles, mercy seat and the veil of the covering.

13. "The table, poles, vessels and the shewbread.

14. "The candlestick for the light, its instruments, lamps and the oil for the light,

15. "And the incense altar, poles, the anointing oil and sweet incense, and the hanging for the door at the entrance of the tabernacle.

16. "Make the altar for burnt offerings with its bronze grate, poles and

vessels, the lavatory and base,

17. "The hangings of the court, pillars, their sockets and the hanging for the door of the court.

18. "The pins of the tabernacle, and the pins of the court and cords.

19. "The vestments of service, the holy vestments for Aaron and the vestments for his sons."

20. And the whole congregation of the children of Israel depart.

21. And everyone who was willing in his heart bring offerings for the Lord God, to do the work of the tabernacle and all its services and for the holy vestments.

22. Both men and women come, as many as are willing-hearted, and bring bracelets and all sorts of jewels of gold; and every man that had set aside an offering of gold brings it to God.

23. And everyone who has blue, purple and scarlet material, and fine linen and goats hair and red skins of rams, and dark blue skins, donate them.

24. Everyone who had set aside silver and brass bring it as an offering for Spirit, and every man who has acacia wood brings it.

25. All the skillful women who do spinning bring what they had spun; blue , purple and scarlet material, fine linen,

26. And goats hair.

27. The princes bring onyx and precious stones,

28. And spices and oil.

29. The people bring a willing offering to God.

30. Moses announces that God has called Bezaliel (Divine sonship), the son of Uri (enlightened), the son of Hur (affirmation of truth) of the tribe of Judah (praise, inspiration, life force).

31. "He has filled Bezaliel with the Spirit of God with wisdom and understanding and with knowledge and all kinds of worksmanship,

32. "To make artistic works, and to work in gold, silver and brass,

33. "And in cutting stones to make any kind of artwork.

34. "And has inspired him to teach, along with Elihab , the son of Ahisamakh (supportive) of the tribe of Dan (Judgment).

35. He has filled both of them with wisdom and inspiration to do carpentry, works of art, embroidery in blue and purple and in fine linen and in scarlet material, and in weaving and any kind of work.

Chapter 36

Bezaliel and Elihab, along with every wise man who knows how to do all manner of work build everything as the Lord God had commanded.

2. Moses inspires Bezaliel, Elihab and all the builders of excellent workmanship.

3. And they receive all that was donated.

4. And the skillful men bring in what they have made each day.

5. They tell Moses that the people bring in much more than is needed.

6. And Moses spreads the word throughout the camp that they were making too many items. So the people stop.

7. They already have enough.

8. The skilled men make ten curtains of fine twined material, with cherubim artistically decorating them.

9. The length of each curtain is 28 cubits (15 yards).

10. They couple five curtains together and the other five together.

11. They make blue loops on the edges of the couplings,

12. They make fifty loops on the edges of each curtain opposite each other.

13. They make fifty clasps of gold and couple the curtains together making one large tabernacle.

14. They make eleven curtains of goats' hair all the same size to provide a roof over the tabernacle.

15. The length of each curtain is thirty cubits (about 50 feet) and width of four cubits (around six and a half feet).

16. They couple five curtains by themselves and six curtains by themselves.

17. They make fifty loops on the edge of the curtain in the coupling and fifty loops on the edge of the curtain which couples the second. (50 became the number of years of a jubilee later on.)

18. They make fifty clasps of brass to couple the tent together, so they

might be one.

19. They make a covering for the tent out of rams' skins dyed red and a covering of badgers' skins above that.

20. They make boards for the tabernacle out of acacia wood, [recognizing Nature's life in trees}, standing up.

21. The length of each board is ten cubits (about sixteen and a half feet) and the breadth one cubit and a half (about 30 inches).

22. Each board has two sockets, one exactly opposite the other.

23. They make twenty boards for the south side of the tabernacle,

24. They make forty sockets of silver under the twenty boards, two per board, and two sockets under another board for its two tenons.

25. And for the north side of the tabernacle, they make twenty boards,

26. And there are forty sockets of silver, two under each board

27. And for the west side they make six boards,

28. They make two boards for the corners on the two sides.

29. They are coupled beneath, and coupled together at the top with one ring. They make both corners this way.

30. There are eight boards with sixteen sockets, two sockets per board.

31. They make bars out of acacia wood;

32. Five bars for the boards on each side.

33. They make a middle bar to pass through the boards from one end to the other.

34. They overlay the boards with gold, and make rings of gold to function as places for the bars, and overlay the bars with gold.

35. They make a veil of blue (peaceful), purple (spiritual) and scarlet (love) material, and fine twined linen with cherubim depicting messengers from God.

36. They make four pillars out of acacia wood and overlay them with gold. Their hooks are made out of gold with sockets made out of silver.

37. They make a hanging for the door of the tabernacle. The material is blue, purple and scarlet and fine twined linen with needlework.

38. They make five pillars of it with their hooks; and they overlay their capitals and fillets with gold; but their five sockets are brass.

Chapter 37

Next, Bezaliel (Divine sonship) makes the ark of acacia wood, two and a half cubits (about fifty inches) long, and one and a half cubits wide (around 30 inches) and a cubit and a half high.

2. He overlays it with pure gold inside and out, and makes a crown of gold for it to go all around.

3. He cast four rings of gold, placing them on all four corners; two on one side and two on the other.

4. He makes poles out of acacia and overlays them with gold.

5. He places the poles through the rings on the sides of the ark to carry

it.

6. He makes the mercy seat of pure gold, two and a half cubits (50 inches) long and one and a half cubits (30 inches) wide.

7. He makes two cherubim of gold for each end of the mercy seat, the seat of the presence of the Divine.

8. He places one cherub on each side of the mercy seat.

9. The cherubim are facing each other with their wings stretching upward to cover the seat.

10. He makes a table out of acacia wood 40 inches long by 20 inches wide and about 30 inches high.

11. He overlays it with pure gold and makes a crown of gold for it

12. He makes a border out of gold, a hand's breadth wide (five inches).

13. He makes four rings of gold and places them at each corner on the feet of the table.

14. The rings are next to the border.

15. He makes the poles of acacia overlaid with gold to carry the table.

16. He makes the vessels for the table as well as the flagons, spoons, cups, and bowls made out of gold for the drink offering.

17. He makes a candlestick cast of one piece of gold including the shaft, branches, bowls, buds and floral decorations.

18. Three branches come out of each side representing the Spirit, Soul and Body of the creative process.

19. Three bowls are fastened to each shaft with buds and flowers.

20. On each candlestick, there are four bowls made to look like almonds with buds and flowers.

21. There are four bowls with buds and flowers. There's a bud under each set of two branches.

22. The buds and branches are identical and the entire candlestick is made out of a piece of molten work.

23. He makes seven lamps and its snuffers and its snuff dishes of pure gold.

24. He makes the candlestick with a talent (equivalent to thousands) of pure gold including all the vessels.

25. He makes the incense altar of acacia; the length being a cubit (19 inches or so), the breadth also a cubit (foursquare), and it's two cubits tall (38 to 40 inches) and its horns are the same

26. It is overlaid with pure gold and the crown is pure gold.

27. There are two rings of gold under its crown by the corners on the two sides for carrying with poles.

28. The poles are acacia overlaid with gold.

29. He mixes the holy anointing oil and the pure incense of sweet spices.

Chapter 38

He makes the altar for burnt offerings out of acacia wood, the length is five cubits (about eight feet) and width, five cubits, so it is foursquare (balanced) and three cubits (about five feet) high.

2. He places horns made of the same material overlaid with brass on the four corners.

3. He makes pots and cauldrons with shovels and hooks and tongs and censers (incense burners) to use on the altar. He makes all the vessels and utensils of brass.

4. He makes a grating for the altar, a network of brass, and places it halfway under the altar.

5. He casts four rings of brass for the grate of brass and places them at the four corners for the carrying poles .

6. He makes the poles out of acacia and overlays them with brass.

7. He places the poles into the rings on the sides of the altar to carry it with them. He makes the altar hollow with boards.

8. He places the brass lavatory and its base of brass at the doorway for the women who will come to pray.

9. He makes the south side of the court with one hundred cubits of fine twined linen (about 160 feet).

10. He makes twenty pillars with twenty bronze sockets. The hooks of the pillars and the fillets are silver.

11. The north side hangings cover 100 cubits (around 160 feet) with twenty pillars and twenty sockets of brass. The hooks of the pillars and the fillets are silver.

12. The west side hangings cover fifty cubits (about 80 feet) with ten pillars and sockets. The hooks of the pillars and the fillets are silver.

13. The east side is also fifty cubits.

14. The hangings of the one side of the gate are fifteen cubits (about 8 feet) with three pillars and sockets.

15. The other side and for the gate of the court there are fifteen cubits on each side (24 feet) with three pillars and sockets.

16. All the hangings for the court are made of fine twined linen.

17. The sockets of the pillars are made of brass; the hooks of the pillars and their fillets are silver; and all the pillars of the court are overlaid with silver.

18. The hanging for the gate of the court is needlework, of blue, purple and scarlet material and fine twined linen, twenty cubits long (about 32 feet) and five cubits in height and width (8 feet).

19. There are four pillars and four brass sockets and silver hooks and silver overlay on the capitals and fillets.

20. All the pins of the tabernacle and court are made of brass.

21. So, these are the dimensions and materials used for the whole tabernacle which houses the ark of the covenant as completed by Moses and the Levites as supervised by Aaron's son, Ithamar,

22. And Bezaliel, the son of Uri, the son of Hur, of the tribe of Judah, all made as God has commanded Moses.

23. Also involved in the work was Elihad, the son of Ahisamakh, of Dan, a carpenter, a craftsman and an embroiderer in blue, purple and scarlet

material, and fine linen.

24. Twenty-nine talents, four hundred thirty shekels of donated gold is used.

25. Silver offerings used total one hundred talents, and one thousand seven hundred, seventy-five shekels.

26. A shekel for every head, or half a shekel by the weighing system of the sanctuary, for everyone who is included in the number over twenty years of age, totaling six hundred three thousand, five hundred fifty men. (Numerologically resulting in the number 10, reduced to a 1, indicating the one God).

27. And the total expenditure is one hundred talents of silver for casting the sockets of the sanctuary and the veil. A hundred sockets are made from one hundred talents, a talent for a socket.

28. It takes one thousand, seven hundred, seventy-five shekels to make hooks for the pillars and overlay for their capitals and overlay for the hooks with silver.

29. The sum total of the brass of the offering is seventy talents, and two thousand and four hundred shekels.

30. With it are made the sockets of the door of the tabernacle of the congregation, and the bronze altar, and the bronze grate for it, and all the vessels of the altar,

31. And the sockets all around the court, and the sockets of the court gate, and all the pins of the tabernacle and the court.

Chapter 39

They make vestments for the service to minister in the sanctuary including the holy vestments for Aaron, as the Lord God has commanded.

2. They make the ephod out of gold, blue, purple and scarlet material and of fine twined linen.

3. The gold is beaten into thin plates and cut into wires worked into the blue, purple and scarlet material and in the fine linen.

4. Shoulder pieces are made and the two edges joined together.

5. They make the embroidered girdle of the ephod that is on it of the same material as God commands Moses.

6. They place the onyx stones in work of gold, engraved with the names of the sons of Israel.

7. Placing them on the should pieces of the ephod as a memorial to the sons.

8. The breastplate is made like the work of an artist using the same material as the ephod: gold, blue, purple and scarlet material and fine twined linen.

9. The breastplate is foursquare, the material doubled, and the size was a span (hand length - from thumb to the tip of the little finger).

10. On it, there are four rows of gems and stones. The first row has sardius (a precious red stone indicating protection and strength), topaz (crystal providing peace), and emerald (clarity of thinking).

11. In the second row is placed carbuncle or garnet (natural energy and protection), a sapphire (purity, serenity, beauty and love) jasper (calmness and grace).

12. In the third row, is Jacinth also known as zircon (beauty, love and peace), carnelian (healing), and an amethyst (serenity and spirituality).

13. In the fourth row, is placed a beryl (peace), onyx (protection) and jasper (calmness and grace).

14. The stones are engraved with the names of the twelve sons of Israel.

15. And there are two chains made of pure gold.

16. And two rings of pure gold are placed on the breastplate and there are two rings on the two ends of the breastplate.

17. Two braided chains of gold are fastened to the ends of the breastplate.

18. And the other two ends of the braided chains are fastened to the two settings and put on the shoulder pieces of the ephod in front of it.

19. Two rings of gold are placed on the two ends of the breastplate on the border of the ephod.

20. Two rings of gold are put on the two shoulder pieces of the ephod underneath toward the front above the embroidered girdle.

21. The breastplate is bound by its rings to the rings of the ephod with a blue lace so it will rest upon the embroidered girdle of the ephod, and the breastplate won't come loose from the ephod.

22. The robe of the ephod is blue (peace).

23. There is an opening in the middle of the top of the robe with a hemmed, woven binding so it won't tear.

24. The hem of the robe is decorated with pomegranates symbolizing fruitfulness, on the blue, purple and scarlet material and fine twined linen.

25. There are bells of gold interspersed between each pomegranate on the hem.

26. There's a golden bell, a pomegranate, a bell, a pomegranate all around the opening on the hem of the robe.

27. They make coats of fine linen of woven work for Aaron and his sons,

28. And a mitre of fine linen, and bonnets of fine linen, and breeches of fine linen,

29. And a girdle of fine twined linen, and blue, purple and scarlet needlework.

30. They make a plate for the holy crown of pure gold and write an inscription on it with the words HOLINESS TO THE LORD GOD.

31. It is tied with a cord of blue to fasten it over the mitre.

32. So, all the work of the tabernacle is finished following the instructions from God given to the children of Israel.

33. They bring the finished tabernacle to Moses, the tent and all its vessels, rings, clasps, boards, pins, bars, pillars and sockets.

34. And the coverings

35. The ark, poles and mercy seat,

36. The table, its vessels and the shewbread,

37. The pure candlestick with its lamps, vessels and the oil for light,

38. The golden altar, anointing oil, sweet incense, and the hanging for the tabernacle door,

39. The altar of brass, its grate of brass, poles and all its vessels, the lavatory and its base,

40. The hangings of the court, its pillars, sockets and the hanging for the court gate, the cords, pins and all the vessels of the service,

41. The vestments for the service and priests,

42. All of this according to what the Lord God commanded Moses.

43. Moses looks upon all the work. Behold, they did it! And Moses blesses them.

Chapter 40

The Lord God says to Moses,

2. "On the first day of the first month, set up the tabernacle.

3. "Put the ark in it with the veil.

4. "Bring in the table and set the things in order to be placed on it; bring the candlestick and light the lamps.

5. "Set up the altar of gold for the incense in front of the ark of the covenant, and fasten the hanging to the entry of the tabernacle.

6. "Set the altar of the burnt offering in front of the door of the

tabernacle.

7. "Set the lavatory between the tent of the congregation and the altar and put water in it.

8. "Set up the court and hang up the hangings at the court gate.

9. "Take the anointing oil and anoint the tabernacle and all that is in it, and sanctify it and all its vessels; it is holy.

10. "Anoint the altar of the burnt offering and all its vessels, and sanctify the altar; it is a most holy altar.

11. "Anoint the lavatory and its base and sanctify it.

12. "Bring Aaron and his sons to the door of the tabernacle of the congregation, and wash them with water.

13. "Put the holy vestments on Aaron and anoint him and sanctify him.

14. "Then bring his sons and clothe them with coats;

15. "And anoint them as you anointed Aaron, and their anointing shall represent the anointing of future generations of the sons of Aaron acting as priests for the people."

16. Moses completes all of this.

17. In the first month of the second year on the first day of the week, the tabernacle is set up.

18. Moses, himself, sets up the tabernacle

19. He spreads the covering over it, symbolizing the overseeing of all people by the Divine.

20. He places the covenant into the ark and pus the poles on the ark and puts the mercy seat above the ark.

21. He brings the ark into the tabernacle and sets up the veil of the door covering and covers the ark.

22. He puts the table in the tent of the congregation on the north side of the tabernacle, outside the veil.

23. He sets the bread on it.

24. He puts the candlestick next to the table on the south side of the tabernacle.

25. He lights the lamps before Adonai, indicating that inner flame of humankind's spiritual nature.

26. He places the golden altar in front of the veil.

27. He burns sweet incense showing the sweet essence of the invisible Spirit always present

28. He set up the hanging at the door of the tabernacle, indicating that we can separate our spiritual awareness from the mundane of the outer world.

29. He puts the altar of burnt offering at the door of the tabernacle and placed a burnt offering and a meal offering on it. This shows the willingness of humankind to give all things to Spirit first.

30. He set the lavatory between the tent of the congregation and the altar and put water in it for washing, the symbol of purification.

31. Moses and Aaron wash their hands and feet in it.

32. The idea is "I now walk on God's Holy ground and the work of my hands I do for God."

33. Moses sets up the court and the altar and hangs the curtains. Moses finishes the work.

34. Then, a cloud covers the tent of the congregation, and the glory of the Lord God fills the tabernacle.

35. Moses isn't able to enter into the tent because the cloud abides on it and the glory of God fills it.

36. When the cloud lifts up from over the tabernacle, the children of Israel continue their journey. When we lift our consciousness we are ready to continue our own spiritual journey.

37. But if the cloud is not lifted, then the journey pauses. (We stay "stuck" and our journey does not continue until the day the cloud is lifted.)

38. For the cloud of the Lord God is upon the tabernacle by day, and fire is on it by night so that all can see the Presence of Spirit through the consciousness of ISIS-RA-EL in all our spiritual journeying.

New Thought Exodus

ABOUT THE AUTHOR

The original author of Exodus is alleged to be Moses, although many scribes and interpreters must have been involved.

Then, Charles Fillmore, co-founder of the Unity School of Christianity in Lee's Summit, Missouri, headed the creation of *The Metaphysical Bible Dictionary.*

From this source and other New Thought books and authors including Dr. Ernest Holmes, the founder of what is now the Centers for Spiritual Living, Reverend Donald Errol Welsh, D.D. compiled *New Thought Genesis* interpreting it line by line so that the reader can compare the Bible verses with this Metaphysical/New Thought version.

Dr. Don was a Broadcast communicator for 23 years having discovered New Thought from a Press Release sent to the radio station where he was the program director. Although the policy of the station was not to air church announcements, the content of the notice mentioned a positive teaching called Unity. That was 1968.

Since then, his spiritual path had led to a group called *Creative Initiative* in the San Francisco Bay area and in 1976, The First Church of Religious Science in San Jose, California. Under the tutelage of Dr. Robert Scott, Dr. Don studied the Science of Mind class work and became a licensed Practitioner of Religious Science in 1983. Scott and Dr. Jack Holland hosted a school of ministry in San Jose, from which Dr. Don graduated in 1987. After an internship at the Religious Science church in Santa Cruz, California, he was awarded a Fellow of Religious Science from Holmes Institute.

Dr. Don served the Ventura County Church of Religious Science where he was ordained in 1992 and served United Churches of Religious Science (now Centers for Spiritual Living) in Miami, Florida, Lancaster, California (The Center of Light) and is presently co-minister with his wife, Rev. LaVonne Rae Andrews/Welsh and the Central Coast Center for Spiritual Living in Templeton, California (northern San Luis Obispo county.)

Contact Dr. Don at donwelsh@sbcglobal.net.

Previous Books

The Mystical 10 – Prospering through Powerful Spiritual Principles

The Mystical 10 – A Workbook to Prosper through Spiritual Tools

New Thought Genesis – Hidden Messages Beyond the Words

Rev. Donald Errol Welsh, DD

Divine Dialogues
With Rev. LaVonne Rae Andrew/Welsh

www.ingramcontent.com/pod-product-compliance
Lightning Source LLC
Chambersburg PA
CBHW062000040426
42447CB00010B/1833